SCREENPRINTING

SCREEN-PRINTING

THE ULTIMATE
STUDIO GUIDE

From Sketchbook to Squeegee

PRINT CLUB LONDON

PRINCETON ARCHITECTURAL PRESS

NEW YORK

Princeton Architectural Press
A McEvoy Group company
202 Warren Street
Hudson, New York 12534
Visit our website at www.papress.com

First published in the United Kingdom in 2017
by Thames & Hudson Ltd, 181A High Holborn,
London WC1V 7QX
© 2017 Print Club London

With thanks to Gunars Prande at the School of Visual Arts in New York for
his invaluable help with the technical terms used in the United States.

Designed by Sarah Boris

For Princeton Architectural Press:
Project Editor: Nicola Brower

Special thanks to: Janet Behning, Nolan Boomer, Abby Bussel, Tom Cho,
Barbara Darko, Benjamin English, Jenny Florence, Susan Hershberg,
Lia Hunt, Mia Johnson, Valerie Kamen, Jennifer Lippert, Kristy Maier,
Sara McKay, Eliana Miller, Wes Seeley, Rob Shaeffer, Sara Stemen,
Paul Wagner and Joseph Weston of Princeton Architectural Press
—Kevin C. Lippert, publisher .

Library of Congress Cataloging-in-Publication Data
Names: Print Club London, author.
Title: Screenprinting : the ultimate studio guide, from sketchbook to
    squeegee / Print Club London.
Description: First edition. | New York : Princeton Architectural Press, 2018.
    | Includes index.
Identifiers: LCCN 2017018367 | ISBN 9781616896553 (alk. paper)
Subjects: LCSH: Serigraphy—Technique.
Classification: LCC NE2236 .P75 2018 | DDC 764/.8—dc23
LC record available at https://lccn.loc.gov/2017018367

Manufactured in China by Imago

INTRODUCTION

Print Club London opened its doors in September 2007 with three beds, the mother of all exposure units, a tin bath as a wash-out unit, a cupboard as an office, a handful of members and a lot of enthusiasm.

After graduating from the BA sculpture course at the Norwich School of Art and Design, Fred Higginson co-founded Bluetack Collective, a fine arts charity that provided art studios at an affordable price for artists working in Norwich. Soon after opening Bluetack, he returned to Dalston in London and set up a second studio, Absorb Arts.

In 2007 Fred met Rose Stallard, a fine art graduate from the Norwich School of Art and Design who was renting space at Absorb Arts and working as a freelance illustrator. Rose, who had a screenprint show at Dazed Gallery in East London, had been working out of Camberwell College of Arts print room. She owned some screenprinting equipment and convinced Fred that what everyone really wanted was a screenprinting studio.

Stallard was part of a growing group of illustrators and designers who were feeling despondent with digital work and felt the need to get back into a studio and physically create work with ink, using their hands.

Higginson had never printed before and had little knowledge of the medium, but by now was very experienced at setting up and running open-access studios. Together they decided to take the plunge and Print Club was born.

The idea was to create an open-access studio. They needed to have enough members to cover the rent and the cost of printing equipment. Print Club was started on a shoestring and they gathered beds, drying racks and equipment from all manner of places. People liked the sound of Print Club and were very generous in donating unused equipment that they didn't have room for. The rest of the kit came from art schools that were closing down their print departments. Ironically, these departments are now reopening. Each of Print Club's beds is named after the place it came from. 'Camberwell Carrot', for example, was bought from Camberwell College of Arts.

The ethos was to create a relaxed studio, somewhere you could rock up on your BMX, print some posters, T-shirts, or band merchandise – it wasn't a space reserved for fine artists. A core value has always been the focus on it being a place to experiment and not worry about making mistakes. Print Club is still to this day a space that is welcoming to everyone, whether they are a seasoned printer or just starting out.

Six months after the studio opened, Fred and Rose were joined by Kate Higginson. Kate had graduated from Central Saint Martins in London and was working in film. After visiting Print Club, and seeing the IOUs and dubious-looking accounts system, she decided to quit film and assist in running the business side of the studio.

The number of members expanded quickly and the brand grew, bringing in lots of exciting projects. Clients ranged from Liberty (the London department store) to Twitter, the Tate galleries, Puma, Nike, Stella McCartney and Disney. The projects varied from live printing on location to printing onto sushi nori paper with edible squid ink. Kate oversaw all aspects of new business and development, expanding collaborations with brands and showcasing artists commercially. This gave Fred and Rose time to work on their own projects as well as meeting new artists, running beginner's workshops and putting on shows such as *Blisters* and Film4 Summer Screen at Somerset House in London.

In July 2008 Print Club put on their first big screenprint show, *Blisters*. Collaborating with lots of up-and-coming and established illustrators and designers, *Blisters* was a big success and launched Print Club into the public arena.

Central to the values of Print Club is making high-quality hand-made limited-edition prints affordable, both to produce and to purchase. This principle guides how the house curates the great and good of the illustrative world. The online gallery became an avenue for all members to sell work and quickly became regarded as one of the players on the East London gallery scene. The reason the Print Club model works is that it not only introduces artists to screenprinting through the weekly workshops, but it also offers them studio space to produce their work and a platform to sell it. It's an organic circle. Print Club now represents more than 500 artists who are proficient in a wide range of techniques and styles, including street art, graphic design and illustration.

By 2012 Print Club had expanded and taken over the entire warehouse on Millers Avenue in Dalston. The final unit contained desk space for designers and freelancers to work and grow their small businesses. Print Club has always focused on working collaboratively with artists in many aspects of their work and the warehouse is testament to how passionate the team is about making a business out of something they love doing. With over 930 sq m (10,000 sq ft) and more than 500 creatives, all supported by the Print Club team, the warehouse is a hive of activity.

printclublondon.com

1st RULE
DO TALK ABOUT PRINT CLUB
2ND RULE
IT'S WATERBASED ONLY
3RD RULE
IF THIS IS YOUR FIRST DAY AT
PRINT CLUB YOU HAVE TO PRINT!

38,000BC

200 AD

1700

1853

1907

1930s

1920s

1940s

1950s

1960s

A SHORT
HISTORY →

MARCO LAWRENCE

A SHORT HISTORY

Marco Lawrence is a British-born printmaker and illustrator
based in New York. He prints commercially for an internationally
renowned selection of artists, museums and institutions.
He is also a successful artist and illustrator in his own right,
with several years' experience teaching printmaking in a
number of studios and colleges in the UK and the USA.

Screenprinting is a stencil-based system of image-making. With the stencilling process, pigment is applied through the open areas of a support or cut-out to create a crisp and repeatable design. The earliest instances of stencilling can be traced back 40,000 years to cave dwellers in southern France, northern Spain and the Indonesian island of Sulawesi. There is evidence that hands were used as a resist to pigments blown at cave walls through a reed or hollow bone.

Paper stencils were used in ancient Egypt, Greece and Rome. A stiff brush was employed to force pigment through the open areas of the stencil or cut-out. These supports are remarkably similar to the type of modern letter or shape stencils that you might find in a hardware shop today. The greatest intrinsic flaw to such stencils is that isolated elements of the cut-out, such as the centre of the letter 'O', must be connected to the outside of the stencil by a branch or bridge to keep them in place. These bridges disrupt the shape and make it difficult to reproduce complex designs.

An ingenious and significant improvement to the manufacture of stencils was the use of threads to support the isolated elements within the design, which removed the need for bridges. The first examples of such use identified to date were during the Song Dynasty in China around 1200 AD. Initially human hair was used to support the stencil, although it was soon replaced by silk thread because of its long filaments and remarkable strength. An entire mesh of threads, stretched over a frame, could then be made to create a screen. This allowed for sophisticated and delicate paper stencils to be supported by the taut mesh, keeping the disparate elements in place while still allowing the pigment to pass between the individual threads.

The process is thought to have reached Europe in the mid-19th century. There are records from both France and England around this time that indicate the use of a mesh of rough silk or bolt cloth stretched across wooden frames to create robust screens. These tolerated brushes forcing dyes and inks through the stencils. Such screens were ideal for printing repeat patterns onto fabric and by the beginning of the 20th century screenprinting had come to dominate the textile trade.

An additional refinement to the process was made in Berlin where, in 1920, Albert Kosloff demonstrated his invention of a rubber-bladed squeegee to force the ink through the stencil, thereby rapidly increasing the rate of repetition.

Screenprinting proved increasingly popular and was adopted by a range of industries, including the sign-writing trade in the USA and for travel and transport posters in Europe. The process received further impetus with the invention of what is arguably its greatest refinement in modern times – the photographic stencil. There is much debate over who first created stencils of this kind, but credit is often given to Roy Beck, Charles Peter and Edward Owens in the USA, who during the 1920s were experimenting with chemicals employed in the Fox Talbot process. Photographic stencils are created using a light-sensitive emulsion applied to the mesh that permits the reproduction of incredibly accurate and faithful images.

Until the mid-20th century the application of the medium had been almost exclusively commercial. However, in the 1950s and 1960s artists working within the Pop Art movement, including key practitioners Andy Warhol, Roy Lichtenstein and Robert Rauschenberg, utilized screenprinting in their practice. Not only did they delight in the potential of the process to generate graphic forms and vibrant colours, but they also adopted screenprinting precisely because of its previous commercial, and indeed industrial, associations.

Today, fine artists, graphic designers and illustrators continue to champion the screenprinting medium. The aesthetic of the process, from bold forms to textured impressions to intentional offset alignment, has become ubiquitous in contemporary creative design. However, it is the beautiful, rich, tactile quality of the prints themselves that arguably makes them so desirable in our increasingly digital world. Regardless of the advances in modern digital printing, this ancient process remains unparalleled in its ability to create impressions of such clarity and definition. Furthermore, it can deliver rich deposits of pigment onto almost any flat surface or substrate.

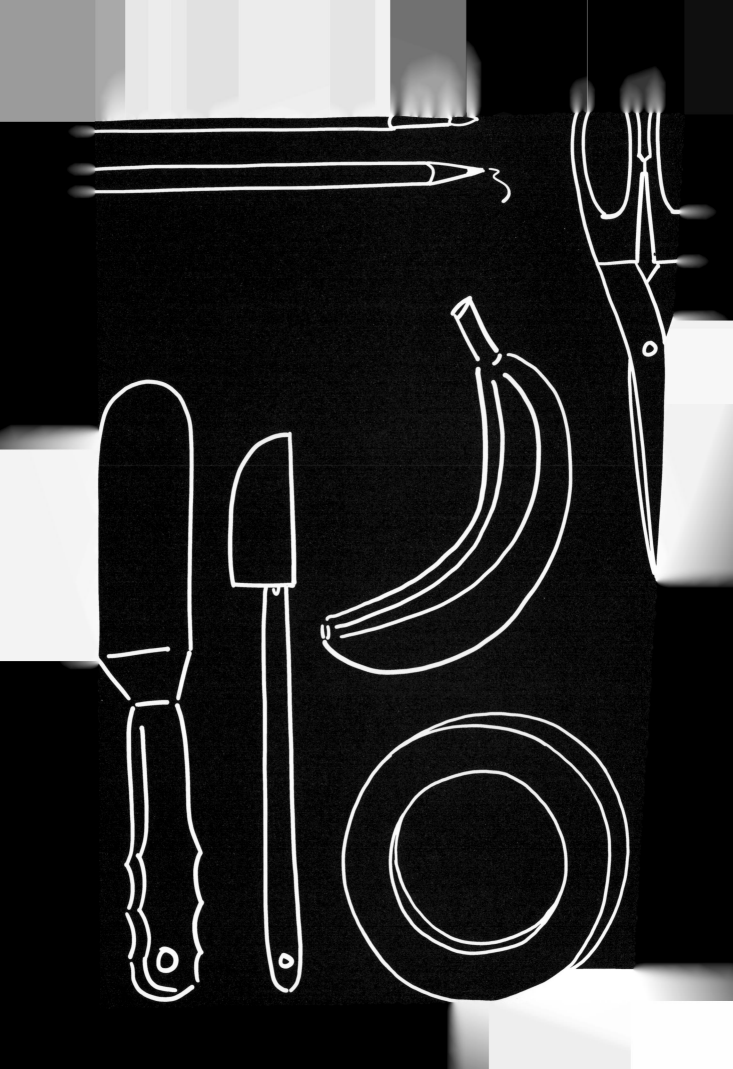

EQUIPMENT

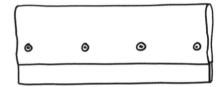

SCREENS

A screen is one of the most important bits of kit for screenprinting (it's in the name). A screen consists of a frame with a tightly woven mesh stretched over it. Most frames used today are metal (aluminium), although some are made of wood. Print Club is a water-based printing studio so the frames are constantly exposed to water when they are being cleaned. Wooden frames can often warp under these circumstances, but an aluminium one won't. The mesh stretched across the frame consists of synthetic polyester threads. Silk was once used (the process was, and still can be, referred to as silk-screenprinting), but it is now easier and cheaper to use a synthetic mesh.

Screens come in all shapes and sizes with various mesh counts: this is how many threads overlap each other per square inch. An average paper-printing screen has a thread count of 90, which means that each square inch of the mesh has 90 very fine threads that overlap each other. With a lower mesh count, the gaps that the ink can pass through are larger and, conversely, with a higher count the gaps are smaller. A low-thread-count screen (between 10 and 50) will be used for printing onto fabrics – anything higher is for printing onto paper. Fabric is very absorbent and so requires a lot of ink to be forced onto

it. Paper, on the other hand, isn't very absorbent and only needs a fine layer of ink to be applied onto it. The lowest thread count screens (between 10 and 20) are used for printing onto very thick fabrics such as hessian sacks. A cotton-printing mesh count would be between 35 and 50. Paper can be printed with anything from a 70 upwards; the average is 90. Paper-printing screens can be up to 120, but anything higher than that can be a struggle to print without a machine because the gaps in the mesh are so fine that an extreme amount of force is required.

POSITIVES

Positives are used to expose an image onto your screen once it has been coated in a layer of emulsion. They can be hand-made or digitally printed, but it's very important that you get them right. If you have a problem with your positive, then you will have a problem when you expose your screen and, no matter how good a printer you are, if your screen is exposed incorrectly, you won't be able to fix it.

The two main rules with a positive are that it is on a transparent paper, which will allow light to pass through it, and that the image you want to apply to your screen is dark enough so that it will block out the UV light during the exposure process. If your positive is a material that doesn't let light through,

then you will just be exposing a shape the size of the paper onto the screen. Similarly, if the image on your positive isn't dark enough and the light can get through, then nothing will be exposed.

With digitally printed positives it is important to make sure that they have been separated properly beforehand. All of the artwork must be pure black (see Digital Separations, page 48). This can then be printed out onto tracing paper, acetate or transparent polyester. Tracing paper is the cheapest, but it doesn't have that much longevity. If, for example, liquids touch it then it can be ruined very easily.

SQUEEGEES

A squeegee is used to force ink through the screen to make a print. They come in all shapes and sizes, but always have two basic parts: the handle and the blade. The handle is often made of aluminium or wood. As with screens, due to constant water exposure, it is better to have a metal handle to avoid warping. The blade is usually made of either rubber, neoprene or polyurethane. Rubber is the most common, but it can degrade much more quickly than neoprene or polyurethane blades if you're using solvents.

Blades come in varying levels of softness and hardness. Generally, a medium hardness squeegee is versatile and can handle most

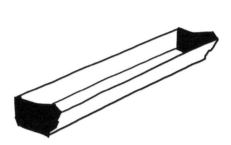

jobs, but a harder squeegee can be used for very fine details on a high-mesh-count screen and a soft squeegee for large ink deposits going down, e.g., with fabric-printing.

The blade itself can come in various shapes. The most common is the square-cut blade, which has a sharp edge and is suitable for most jobs. With paper-printing, especially, the blade needs to have a nice sharp corner so that a very thin surface area is pushing ink through the mesh. If the blade is curved, or dull, too much ink can be forced through, which will result in your image 'bleeding' on your paper. Curved and D-cut (sometimes referred to as V) squeegees allow more ink to pass through the screen due to a larger surface area. These are used for fabric-printing. However, a square-cut blade is also frequently used in fabric-printing. The angle that the squeegee is held at is very important in printing. Generally, the squeegee should always touch the screen at a 45-degree angle (see The Basics of Printing on Paper section, page 56).

EMULSION

A photo-emulsion is used to make the stencil on the screen. The type of emulsion you will need may depend on what you are printing with. For instance, as Print Club is a water-based printing studio, it is important that the emulsion is resistant to water-based inks. Emulsion is a light-sensitive chemical that is first applied to the screen using the scoop coater and is then left to dry. If water then touches the emulsion, it will run off the screen. The chemical hardens when exposed to a powerful UV light and can only then be removed from the screen with a chemical stencil stripper. It is normally supplied in two parts: the emulsion and then an activator (or sensitizer) chemical that makes the emulsion sensitive to UV light. Once 'activated', it does have a shelf life and won't last forever. It comes in all colours, but green is the most common at Print Club.

SCOOP COATER

This piece of kit is very simple but extremely important because it is used right at the start of the print process. The scoop coater is used to apply a thin layer of emulsion onto the screen. Usually a scoop coater is metal with plastic caps to allow for ease of cleaning. The scoop coater needs to have a smooth straight edge to coat a screen evenly and smoothly – if there are any dents in the scoop coater, then streakiness can occur when coating. The scoop coater should always be thoroughly cleaned after use. It's also useful to have a few different sizes of scoop coater to match your screens. The scoop coater should be roughly 2 cm (¾ in.) thinner each side than the mesh you are printing on. If it overlaps onto the frame, then sometimes an uneven coating can occur. It's best to use a smaller one to get an even coverage of emulsion and to use packing tape later on in the process to cover the edges up.

INK

Inks can either be bought pre-made ready for printing or can be mixed using acrylic inks and a screenprinting medium. The medium increases the drying time of an acrylic ink and thins it out so it won't dry up while the ink is sitting on the screen. It will be just viscous enough to be pushed through the mesh. Many inks have their own properties and it's important to experiment to find the right ones. While colour is obviously key, you should also consider transparency with screenprinting inks. Sometimes an ink can look much richer in colour when it is in a container compared to when it has been printed. Generally, lighter colours are more transparent than darker colours because of the difference in richness of the pigment used to make them. For example, black inks tend to be very opaque and will sit on top of most colours without letting any other colour show through, but if a yellow is printed on top of many colours, then the layers below will probably show through. Using transparent inks in screenprinting is key to creating overlays (see page 172).

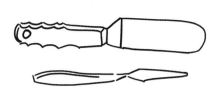
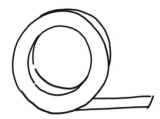

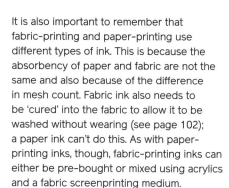

It is also important to remember that fabric-printing and paper-printing use different types of ink. This is because the absorbency of paper and fabric are not the same and also because of the difference in mesh count. Fabric ink also needs to be 'cured' into the fabric to allow it to be washed without wearing (see page 102); a paper ink can't do this. As with paper-printing inks, though, fabric-printing inks can either be pre-bought or mixed using acrylics and a fabric screenprinting medium.

CLOTH
A cloth can be used to clean your screen and to wipe up any pesky ink spillages you may get on your print bed. Always give it a little wash after use and try not to use one that has too many fibres on it that could come off onto your screen when cleaning.

PALETTE KNIVES
These come in all shapes and sizes and it's always a good idea to have a range. They usually have a wooden handle with a thin metal blade protruding from it. They are vital for mixing inks and for efficiently removing ink from your screen. The best ones tend to have a fairly wide curved blade, allowing it to glide over the mesh when removing ink, while at the same time keeping the ink away from your hand.

ACETATE
A sheet of acetate is used during the registration process (see page 88). It should always be cleaned after use so that it stays transparent, or it will be hard to register with.

SCRAP PAPER
This is used to test that your design is printing through your mesh properly. You don't want to start printing straight onto your edition paper, as you can end up wasting sheets on mistakes that can be fixed on scrap paper. Newsprint can be good to print on as a test, especially after cleaning a screen, as it is very absorbent and can help to clear any excess water from the mesh. It's always good to have enough scrap paper to hand when printing – you don't want to be running around trying to grab something to print onto if you've run out of paper.

SWEETS
If you are having a late-night print session and need some energy, then sweets are essential.

PANTONE SWATCH BOOK
A swatch book is a collection of colours with reference codes to match. It is vital when mixing inks (see page 70).

DUCT TAPE
This can be used to fix holes that may appear in your mesh. It is important with mesh that it stays taut. If you have any big holes, then you will probably need to get your screen re-meshed. However, duct tape can be used to cover up any little holes so your mesh will keep going a little bit longer.

PACKING TAPE
Packing tape is used to cover up any part of your screen that the emulsion doesn't cover. It does the same job as the emulsion in that it blocks out ink from passing through the mesh, but it tends to be used only on the outside of the frame where the scoop coater can't reach.

CUP OF TEA
This is an absolute must and perfect when having a rest in between printing the layers.

SCISSORS
Scissors have a multitude of uses throughout printing, from cutting up scrap paper and positives through to trimming down registration marks.

ELECTRONIC SCALES
Used for mixing up inks (see page 70).

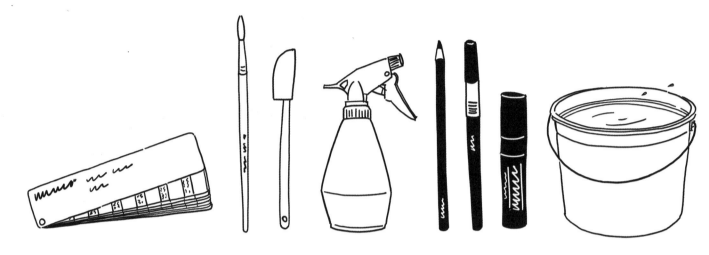

PHONE
Not an absolute must but useful if it has a calculator on it. It can also be used to play some killer jams while you're printing and to Instagram some sneak peaks of your fantastic work.

CONTAINERS
Used for mixing up inks.

WATER SPRAY
Handy for cleaning your screen during printing. A light application can be used if needed and it means that the water is always clean.

APRON
Extremely useful if you're a messy printer.

PAINT BRUSH
Good for painting emulsion onto your screen when pin-holing (see page 68).

PENS / LITHOGRAPHIC PENCIL
A variety of drawing tools mainly used for fixing any mistakes in your positives, or even creating your positives from scratch.

MASKING TAPE
Masking tape has a variety of uses, from sticking your positives onto your paper for registration purposes to attaching to paper to make registration marks.

REGISTRATION MARKS
These are normally thick pieces of paper cut down to size with masking tape attached to them, although you can buy sticky plastic ones that stay very firmly planted to the table. They are used to act as a guide to slot your paper into when printing.

RULER
Handy for making sure your positives are stuck onto your paper straight and centred for registration purposes.

BANANA
Slightly healthier than sweets. A good source of energy when printing late into the night.

SPRAY MOUNT
Used for fabric-printing to stick T-shirts, tote bags, or fabric down onto the platen.

COCONUT WATER
A great refreshing treat at the end of a long print session.

SPONGE
Used to clean off your screen after exposing, and also during the print process if you need to clean your screen at any point.

CARDBOARD SQUARES
Useful for cleaning excess emulsion off the edges of your screen.

BUCKET
Keep a bucket of clean water next to you when printing in case you need to clean your screen.

BEER
The BEST way to end a long print session. Good job!

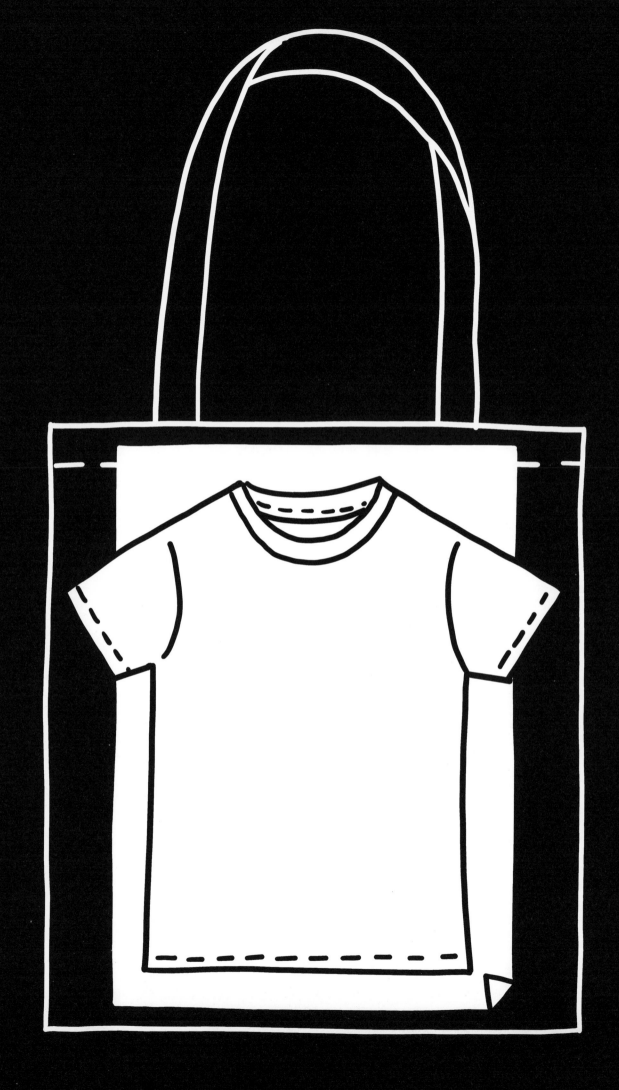

MATERIALS

PAPER

You can screenprint onto almost anything, but paper is undeniably the most common material. As it isn't very absorbent, it is an ideal medium for screenprinting. You only need a very fine layer of ink for it to sit smoothly on top of the paper, but choosing which sort of paper to print on can be a tough decision. A good design should always be printed onto a high-quality paper, one that isn't too thin and has longevity. Many printers use a variety of papers that often relate to their artwork; for example, prints that are considered more abstract or to be 'fine art' are frequently printed on deckled-edge paper that is usually a bit thinner, softer and textured, while a contemporary illustration or graphic art is normally printed on smoother paper with a straight edge.

Weight is an important factor when thinking about how much ink will be printed onto the paper. For example, with a thinner stock the paper can often warp when large amounts of spot colour are printed. A weight around 300gsm is advisable for printing, although it really is a question of the printer's preference. Colour is also something to consider. Although prints are mostly made on white or just off-white paper, a different-coloured paper can also be used. This can save time when printing and create some really interesting effects when taking the transparency of inks into account. As with most materials in screenprinting, it's important to experiment with different paper options to find what works for you.

TEXTILES

Cotton rather than anything synthetic is generally used when screenprinting onto fabric. People mostly choose to print onto T-shirts or tote bags, but also onto tea towels, cushion covers, curtains and large lengths of fabric that can be made into clothes. Fabric is very absorbent, so a lot of ink needs to be forced into it – anything synthetic will stop the ink settling into the material and it will sit on top. If this happens, then general wear will result in the ink flaking off the material. The studio at Print Club prints using water-based inks, but the fabric is cured at extremely high temperatures after it is printed so that the ink can react and settle into the fabric. This then means that water can touch it without displacing it from the fabric.

In terms of preparing a screen, the process is the same as paper-printing (see page 60), but the printing process is different – the equipment needed isn't the same and slightly different techniques are used. There are a few more limitations surrounding fabric-printing as well. There is a limit on the number of layers depending on the kind of screenprinting press you are using.

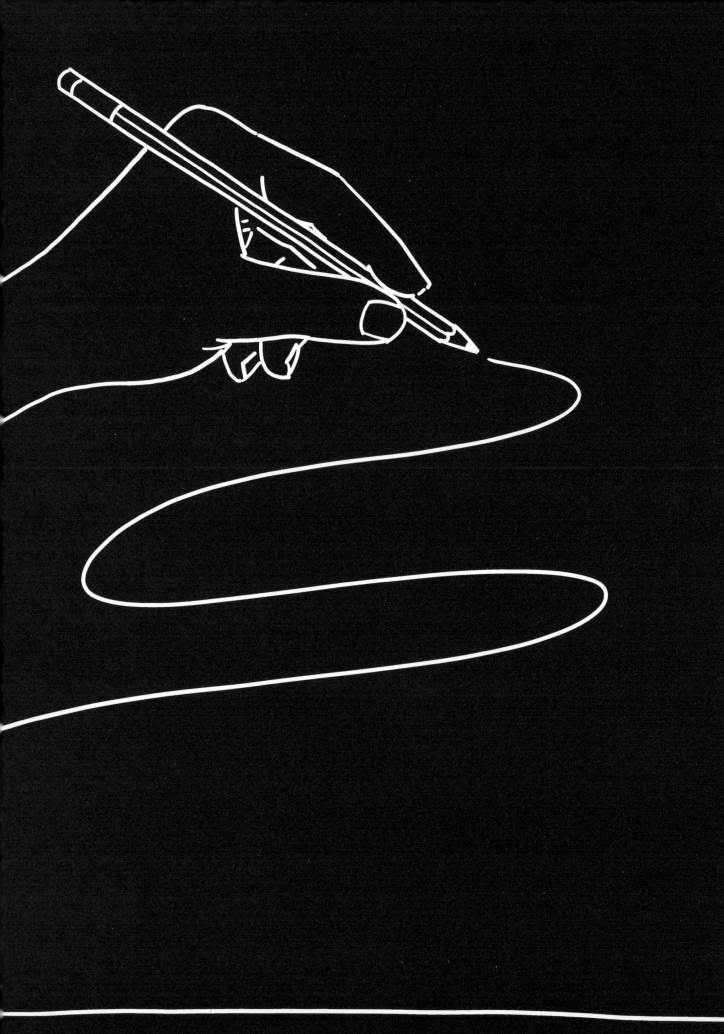

ARTWORKING
YOUR DESIGN

ROSE STALLARD

ARTWORKING YOUR DESIGN

London-based illustrator Rose Stallard is the creative director and co-founder of Print Club. Splitting her time between Print Club, commissioned work and her own projects, the iconic illustrator brings the Print Club brand to life with her inimitable 1970s fanzine-style artworks and edgy typography. Everything Stallard does, from curating new talents to producing exclusive artworks for the gallery, is injected with a little hint of rock 'n' roll.

'The first stage of the screenprinting process is making your artwork. This chapter will show you how to get your artwork ready to be exposed onto a screen. The first part shows you how to ditch your computer and go old school, using a mixture of rubylith and hand-drawn artwork to make your positives. Forget the undo button and enjoy the time this process gives you to think. In the second part you'll see how to artwork the same design digitally. Many artists mix and match the processes for ease and a more hand-finished feel. Have fun!'

USED TO BELONG TO ZIGGY
HE PLAYED IT LEFT HAND
GUITARS I HAVE KNOWN
NUMBER 4
A/P

ANALOGUE ARTWORKING

There are lots of techniques that can be used to make positives for screenprinting and there isn't necessarily a set correct way to make them. This section will give you an insight into how to make your own positives from scratch, using a combination of hand-cut and hand-drawn positives together.

Step 1 – You will need masking tape, double-sided tape, a stencil knife (a barrel-handed knife is best), new blades, scissors, a ruler, an opaque marker pen, a pencil, rubylith, vellum, cardboard and register pins and tabs. (If you don't have register pins and tabs, you can use masking tape.)

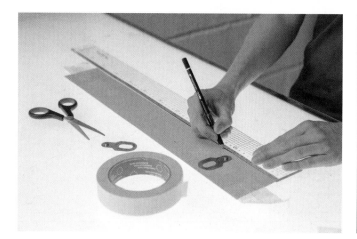

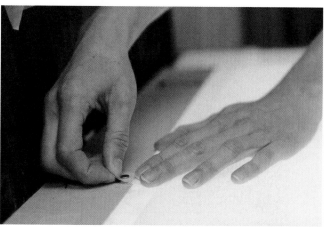

Step 2 – Attach your register pins to a strip of cardboard using masking or packing tape. The register pins either have plastic tabs that can be attached to your positive or they can be inserted directly into your positive through holes made by a standard-size hole punch. These tabs can even be hand-made. Make the cardboard the same width as your positives to help you work out where the pins should go. Tape the card securely to your light box.

Step 3 – Attach a thin piece of double-sided tape onto the end of the plastic tab not attached to the pin. Clip two plastic tabs over the registration pins. Lay your cut-to-size drawing film onto the light box just below the cardboard strip. Once it looks straight and is in position, peel off the double-sided tape and attach the tabs to the drawing film. Each time a positive is made, you can attach your film by laying it over the positive below. Don't worry if you don't have register pins, you can use masking tape to secure your positives to the light box. It's just a bit harder to move them around.

Step 4 – The first positive is the black layer. Stallard didn't want the cut-out feel of rubylith for this layer so she opted to hand-draw it instead. This means her final positives will be a combination of hand-drawn and hand-cut elements. The line work is hand-drawn onto the drawing film using an opaque black paint pen. You can work away from the light box if you prefer because you have your tabs attached to your drawing film. You can place your original drawing or rough under your film or pencil on your design first. (Remember to rub out any pencil marks once you have redrawn.) If you make a mistake, you can use an eraser pen designed to remove ink or very carefully scratch away with a stencil knife.

Step 5 – Cut a sheet of rubylith, making it slightly smaller than the hand-drawn layer. With the satin side up, and making sure it is flat, attach this to your hand-drawn layer using double-sided tape. (Three small pieces down each side is enough.)

Step 6 – Using a sharp stencil knife (a barrel-handed knife is best), gently cut away the area that does not need to be black. Cut in between the black outline of the hand-drawn positive so that the actual printed line is the hand-drawn line and not the cut line.

Step 7 – Carefully peel away the top layer of the rubylith from its clear backing sheet. Cut and peel a bit at a time to avoid making mistakes. If you do make a mistake, get a scrap piece of rubylith, carefully peel the backing off and reapply it to the area you need to recut.

Step 8 – It is good practice to keep a note of the colour of each layer on the tabs of each positive, especially if you're making a print with many layers.

Step 9 – To make the positive for the pink layer, first cut the rubylith to size. The width is the same, but only cut to the length that you need. Lay the rubylith satin side up over the black layer positive and then fix the tabs in the same way as in Step 1. This is now lined up and ready to be cut.

Step 10 – The following layers will all need trapping. Although the black layer has been cut first, the coloured layers will sit below this when printed and consequently will need trapping added. Instead of cutting between the line, Stallard now cuts a good 3 to 5 mm (around ¼ in.) outside of the black drawn line. Manually adding trapping will always be a bit inconsistent, whereas digitally adding it (see page 52) will create a more uniform trapping.

TIPS

Trapping is an overlap of colour placed on the first/lightest layers of a print. Printing darker, more opaque colours on top will then generally mean the white of the paper won't show through even if there is some slight mis-registration in the print. For example, on this print, making the blue letters slightly bigger than they need to be, and keeping the black top layer the same as the blue, means they will appear to be printed perfectly.

Step 11 – Carefully peel away the top layer of the rubylith from the clear backing sheet as in Step 7.

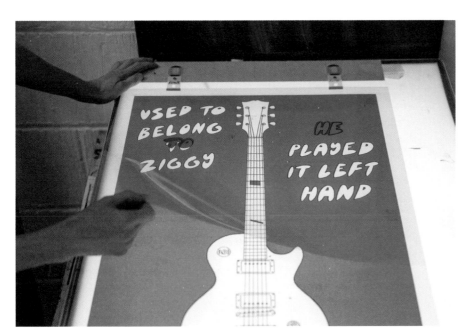

Step 12 – The pink layer is finished. You can see how the trapping will sit under the black layer when it is printed.

Step 13 – Get your black, pink, red, yellow and blue layers ready. For the final layer, which is going to be white, attach another layer of drawing film. You can use anything that's transparent since you're not going to draw on it.

Step 14 – Rather than cutting this layer out of the rubylith, which would look hand-cut, the type is hand-drawn. It is best to draw onto a new sheet of drawing film cut to the size you need, so that if you make a mistake you can have another go!

Step 15 – If you were doing this digitally, you would not need this extra layer, as you would just select the type in Photoshop and cut it out of the black layer. However, because the type is quite fine here, an additional white layer will be printed on top of the black. Working in an analogue fashion sometimes means a little bit more labour.

Step 16 – Stick the hand-drawn type with masking tape to the transparent sheet added in Step 13. Once it is positioned in the correct place, use double-sided tape to secure it properly. Then remove the masking tape.

Step 17 – To add registration marks, put a cross in the same place on each positive. If you were taping down your positives, you would need to do this as you went along, but if you are using the registration pins, you can do it at the end.

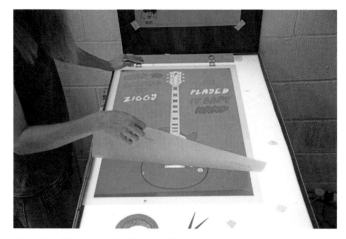

Step 18 – Here are all of the positives made using hand-drawn layers and rubylith. They are all ready to expose as normal.

Step 19 – Once all the screens have been exposed, they are ready to be printed. The first to print is the blue layer.

Step 20 – These are the red and pink layers.

Step 21 – Next is the yellow. Every new layer has been registered to the original rubylith positive using the registration markers made earlier on the positives.

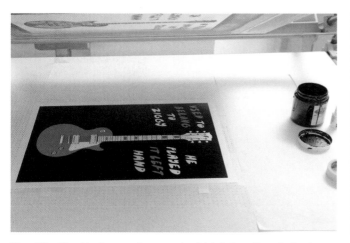

Step 22 – The black goes down next, which brings the whole piece together.

Step 23 – A final white layer is now printed using a very opaque ink on top of the black because of the analogue process used.

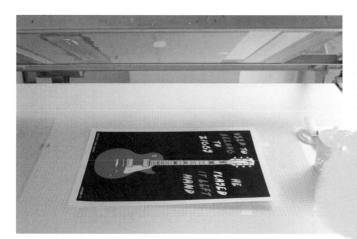

Step 24 – This is the final piece.

TIPS

Registration marks are little markers (normally crossheads in each corner of your design) that will be exposed onto your screen and used in the print process to align all of your layers. Although they are exposed, you won't print them in your final edition. They are often used when elements on a print are 'floating' on a page and don't necessarily touch each other. This would be very tricky without registration markers as a guide for the printer. Normally they are printed once onto your paper and then covered up with tape so they won't be printed. You will need to repeat the process on all of the layers, covering up the markers after the first print each time. In the end, you will have one print that has a printed marker from each layer, but they won't appear on the rest of the edition.

These materials can be used to make hand-made positives. On the left is the mark made on a sheet of tracing paper and on the right is a screenprint made using the tracing paper positive. As you can see, the thicker ink-based pens such as the POSCA pen or film marker give you an almost 1:1 representation of what the finished print will look like. Using painted ink or a lithographic pencil can result in some inconsistencies in printing, but they do create a very nice texture that is hard to achieve digitally. Experimenting with exposure times can help a lot when using hand-made positives. For example, less light would be required for thinner markers or pencils, as too much light can result in an overexposed image. For tips on exposing see The Basics of Printing (page 56).

DIGITAL SEPARATIONS

Creating positives digitally can seem a bit daunting at first, but by learning a few small techniques a lot can be achieved. In this section you can turn an image already created into something print-ready by using Photoshop. Photoshop is one of the most commonly used pieces of software for digital separations and, with even limited knowledge of the program, you should be able to follow the steps here.

For some more advanced digital separations techniques, check out the artist spotlights for Matthew Green: Halftone (page 162) and Thomas Whitcombe: Photo to CMYK (page 206).

Step 1 – Create your artwork using Photoshop. The artwork has five
layers, one for each of the colours of the print.

Step 2 – Lowering the opacity of the top black layers means you can
see that the colours align perfectly, with no overlaps. However, as in
the analogue process, some trapping is going to be needed here.

Step 3 – Start by clicking on the selection wand – a key tool that will enable you to create an even layer of trapping around any shape. This is where having all of your print layers on separate Photoshop layers will come in handy. Starting with the blue layer, use the selection wand to click on the L of the word left.

Step 4 – Highlight all of the letters on this layer. To add to your existing selection, simply hold down SHIFT while using the selection wand and click on the other elements on the same layer.

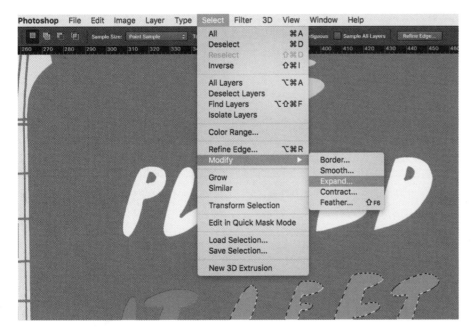

Step 5 – Once you've selected the whole word, then click on SELECT > MODIFY > EXPAND.

Step 6 – The EXPAND option allows you to increase your selection by a designated number of pixels. On this piece three pixels have been used, but the number selected will be entirely dependent on your own artwork.

Step 7 – Once the selected letters have been expanded, you will need to fill in the empty part of the selected area. You can use either the BUCKET or BRUSH tool.

Step 8 – Once filled in, it is clear that with the transparent black layer on top the blue is bigger than it needs to be. This means it has sufficient trapping to print.

Step 9 – Once you are happy that a layer is finished, then it's time to prepare it to be printed as a positive. This means turning everything on the layer entirely black so that when it is printed on transparent paper it will expose perfectly onto the screens. BITMAPPING is a digital process that will turn everything on the screen into either pure black or white. It is commonly used when preparing positives digitally. First make the desired layer the only visible one (this process will need to be repeated for all of the layers).

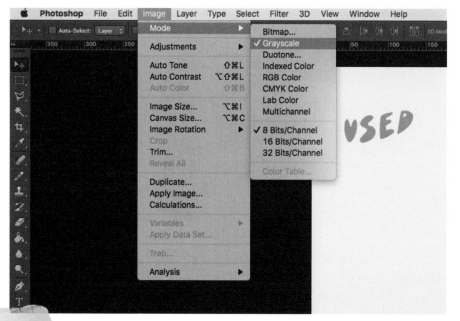

Step 10 – Click on IMAGE > MODE > GREYSCALE and then flatten the layers. You will have to repeat this process for all of the layers.

Step 11 – Using one method of BITMAPPING, the tone of grey on the image needs to be over 50%. The EYEDROPPER tool shows that this is 44% grey; 0% is white and 100% is pure black. Once BITMAPPED, everything on screen will be one of those values.

TIPS

This method of BITMAPPING is called 50% threshold. All the pixels on screen that are 50% grey or less are made white and any pixels above that value will be made 100% black. If done correctly, this method will ensure that everything on screen that you need is 100% black and when printed on a positive it will expose properly onto your screen.

Step 12 – To make the image darker (over 50% in terms of the scale from black to white) click on IMAGE > ADJUSTMENTS > LEVELS.

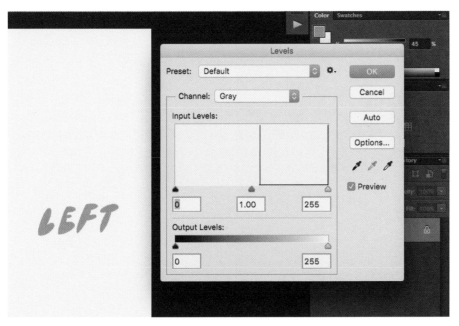

Step 13 – LEVELS help lighten or darken the image using a white, grey and black slider.

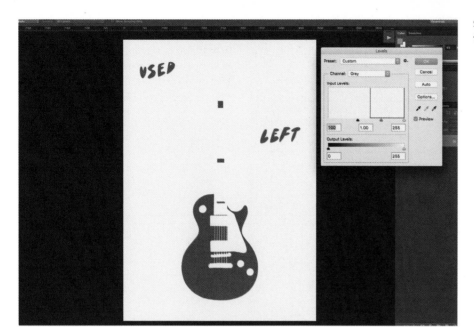

Step 14 – Adjusting the black slider makes the image much darker.

Step 15 – The EYEDROPPER tool shows that the tone is 77% grey. Now you can BITMAP the image.

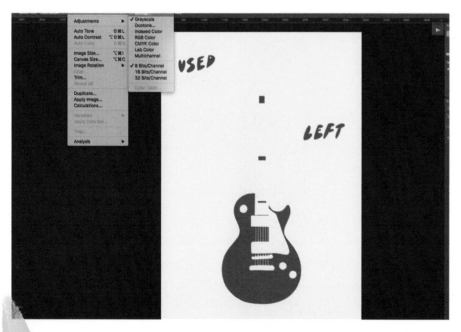

Step 16 – Click on IMAGE > MODE > BITMAP.

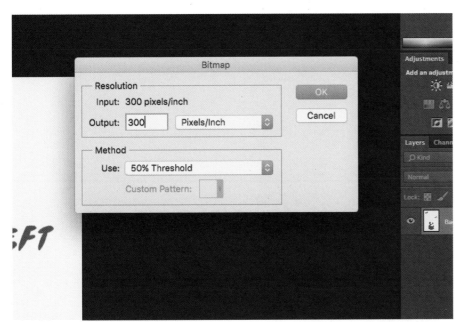

Step 17 – Normally you should make artwork at 300 dpi and BITMAP it at the same resolution. Select 50% threshold under METHOD. Everything that is 50% black and above will be made pure black and everything else will be made white.

Step 18 – The parts of your image that were over 50% on the white–black scale have now turned fully black. You can check by using the EYEDROPPER tool.

Step 19 – If you zoom in, you can see there are no grey pixels, just black and white. This will ensure that when printed out onto tracing paper or acetate, all UV light is blocked out when exposing. This will yield a clean edge stencil to print with. You will need to save this image separately to your original file and then go back to the beginning to repeat the process for all of the layers. These are now ready to send to the printer. PDFs are normally the recommended file type.

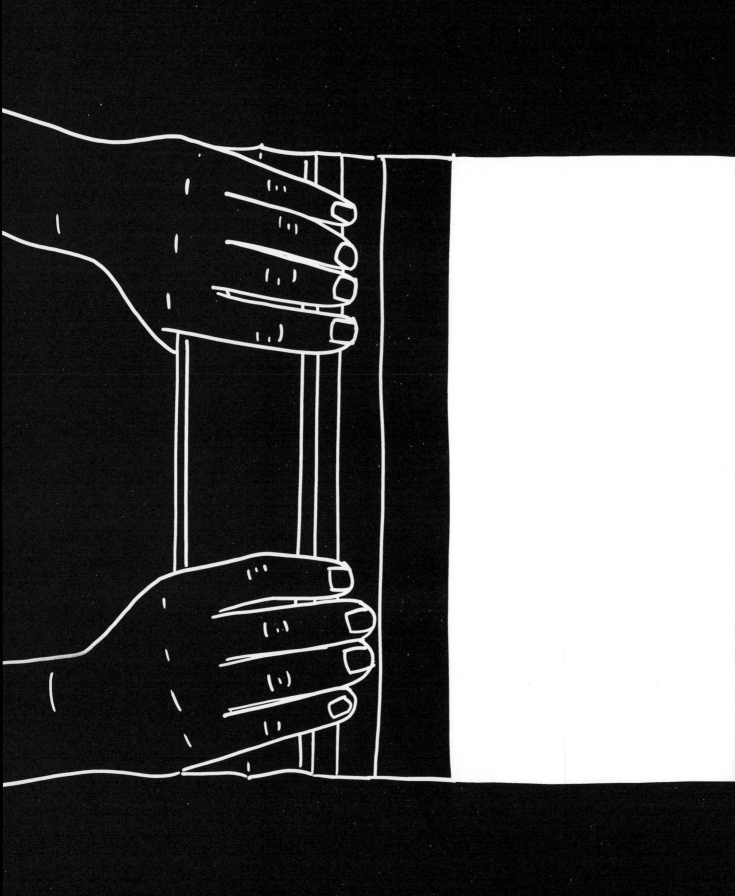

THE BASICS
OF PRINTING
ON PAPER

FINALIZING YOUR POSITIVES

Your positives should appear black on a clear sheet of acetate, polyester film or tracing paper. This black will block out the light of an exposure unit against your screen and stop the desired areas of emulsion from hardening into your screen. Remember, you will need a positive for each layer in your design.

Grey colours will not transfer onto a screen during the exposure process. Check the previous chapter for tips on optimizing digital work for screenprinting.

Step 1 – Often printers can miss out small bits of black ink from positives, especially on large areas. It is always useful to place the positive on top of a light box and check for any mistakes. If you notice ink missing in any areas, you can rectify this using a pure-black marker pen. You can also check for tips on hand-drawing positives on page 202.

TIPS

Make sure you are using a pure-black pigment pen and that it's dry. If you've drawn something and instantly taken it to the exposure unit, the ink may still be wet and it will be smudged off your positive.

Ensure you are using the correct tool on the correct textured positive. For example, using a lithographic pencil on acetate won't yield good results.

Step 2 – Flip the positive over so the back is face up and draw over the areas missing ink. By drawing on the back, you don't risk removing any of the printed ink on the reverse side. Remember that the positive you are looking at is what is going to be exposed onto the screen. If you aren't happy with it or there is a mistake on it, then it's going to be hard to resolve after exposing.

Halftone images can be quite hard to fix if a printer has made a mistake. This is because halftone is such a precise computer process that when you try to fix it with your hands, it is often very noticeable. It may be better to try to get it reprinted properly.

If you notice any errors, or get any bits of mess on your positive (something that can happen in a busy studio), you can simply cut it away.

Make sure that any ink from a pen has properly dried before taking your positive over to the exposure unit.

SETTING UP YOUR SCREEN

Learning how to prepare screens efficiently is essential for creating clean and consistent print editions. No matter how good a printer you are, if your screen isn't prepared properly, things are going to go wrong. It's worth taking your time and familiarizing yourself with this process. The better your screen is made, the easier it is going to be when you are printing.

If printing a multi-layered print, then it is advisable to make all your screens up together to save yourself time. This whole coating process should take place in a red-lit room so that UV light isn't touching the emulsion. You can buy a light-safe darkroom bulb and minimize the amount of natural light that could hit your screen if you don't have a red-lit room.

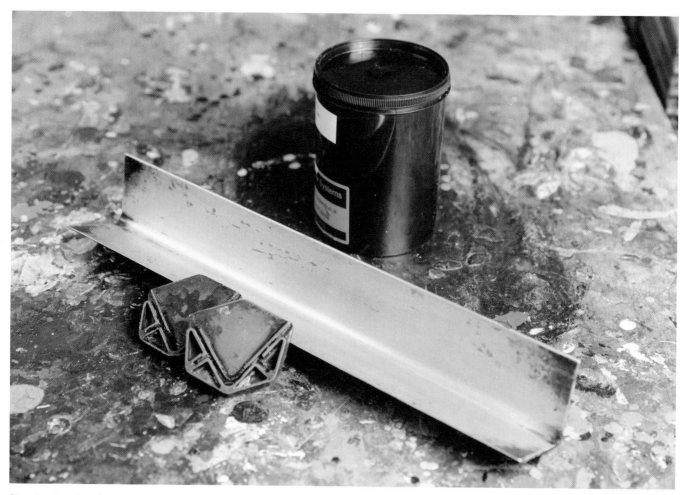

Step 1 – The first step is to coat your screen in emulsion. Make sure it is activated before you start (see Emulsion, page 25). To coat your screen use a scoop coater. Make sure it is clean and free of dust because you don't want dust to get into the emulsion. If it does, then it will transfer onto the screen and can cause problems down the line (see the information about pin-holes on page 68).

Step 2 – Fix the ends to the main body of the scoop coater with brown packing tape to make sure that no emulsion leaks out of the sides. Be careful that the tape doesn't touch either of the top edges of the scoop coater as it can interfere with the coating process.

Step 3 – Before coating your screen, make sure it is free of hair and dust by gently rubbing over the mesh with your hand. This will reduce the amount of pin-holes (see page 68) in your stencils and ultimately save you having to fix mistakes later on.

Step 4 – Place your screen against a wall at a slight angle. It is helpful to use something to hold the screen in place while coating. At Print Club the wooden slats at different heights allow frames of all sizes to slot into the wall and stay secure.

TIPS

It may be that your screen has lost tension and so dips slightly in the middle. This means that more emulsion can gather there when coating. If this happens, you could try using a slightly smaller scoop coater or, alternatively, you may need to get your screen restretched.

Step 5 – It's time to open up the emulsion. Pour it into the scoop coater until it is at least a quarter full. Don't be worried about using too much as the excess will go back in the container once you've coated your screen.

TIPS

Make sure that the scoop coater you are using has a smooth, straight edge. Any kinks in it can result in too much emulsion being applied to certain areas and streaks down your screen after coating.

Step 6 – Make sure that all of the emulsion is evenly distributed in the scoop coater, with no side clearly having more in it. Place the scoop coater about 5 cm (2 in.) above the bottom of the mesh (not the frame) and gently tip the scoop coater forward until all of the emulsion has touched the mesh. This will result in a more even coating over the screen.

Step 7 – When you are sure that all of the emulsion has hit the mesh, firmly lift the scoop coater up the screen, making sure the scoop coater touches the mesh at all times. Don't rush this part – do it slowly.

Step 8 – Stop around 5 cm (2 in.) from the top of the mesh. While applying pressure on the screen gently tilt the scoop coater down and allow any excess emulsion on the mesh to fall back into it. Gently push the scoop coater up on the mesh and pull away. This will stop any emulsion dripping down the screen. This part of the process can be tricky.

The aim is to get a nice even coat of emulsion on the screen. If you notice any inconsistencies or if any emulsion has dripped down the screen, don't panic. This can be fixed. Simply take the scoop coater back to the bottom, press it against the mesh and firmly glide it up the screen. Don't apply any more emulsion this time though, just use the scoop coater to scrape the excess off the screen.

Step 9 – When coating, emulsion can often get pushed to the side, leaving a thick track of it. This will increase the drying time of the screen and it can be harder to clean off at the end. Using a small piece of paper, glide it up the screen to remove the emulsion. Once coated, it is important that you don't touch the emulsion, as this can ruin the stencil before you can even expose.

Step 10 – The screen is then placed horizontally in a dark, heated cupboard. Exposure to a little bit of light normally happens at this stage, but it shouldn't affect the emulsion if done hastily. Storing the screen horizontally will keep the emulsion layer spread consistently all over.

Step 11 – Going back to the coating area, you should now decant the remaining emulsion back into the container from the scoop coater. Pop off one of the ends and tilt the scoop coater into the tub. Using a bit of card you can easily glide any excess back in so you can use it next time. The more you save, the longer your emulsion will last!

TIPS

Be diligent with your emulsion! If dust or hairs have got into it, then every time you coat your screen it's going to be covered in debris. When you're decanting emulsion back into the tub after use be sure to use clean materials and check that the emulsion that's been used doesn't look as though it has hair or dust in it. Also, be careful if you're drying your screen outside because it may collect a lot of dust.

Step 12 – Once your screen is dry to the touch, it's time to expose. The emulsion at this point is sensitive to the light and is not hardened. If it is hit with water, it will run off the screen. Certain areas will be hardened using UV light and some parts will be blocked from the light using the positive. After exposing, you can clean away the emulsion that you kept from the light to create the stencil. At Print Club the large exposure unit is fitted with a high-wattage UV bulb for speedy exposure times. However, you can use a standard flood light if you do not have access to an industrial model.

Step 13 – Before using the exposure unit, it's best to give the glass a clean. If a screen that isn't entirely dry is exposed, hardened emulsion can sometimes be left on the glass afterwards and it will expose onto your screen. Make sure the glass is shimmering clean using glass cleaner, a rag and a razor blade to scrape the stubborn bits off.

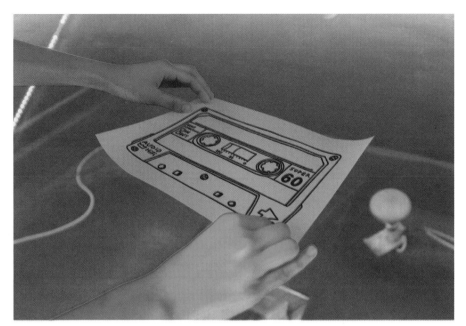

Step 14 – Now it's time to place your positive onto the glass. It is important to lay it down on the glass face up, so you are looking at it as you would when it's printed. If you accidentally put it in backwards and expose your screen, then you have no choice but to start again.

Step 15 – The exposure unit is fitted with a vacuum. This is very important as you need the glass of the unit, the positive and the mesh of the screen to all be flat against each other. If there is even a slight gap between them, you run the risk of exposing a blurry stencil onto your screen, as the light will hit your positive and lose its sharpness by travelling through the gap between the screen and the mesh. If you don't have a vacuum, then a heavy object such as a book can be used instead to make everything sit nice and flush.

Step 16 – Placing a hollow tube half in the screen and half out will aid the vacuum in sucking the air out of the inside and force the positive and the mesh together to give a clean exposure. Now you can close the lid of the exposure unit and check the settings. You need to ensure that enough light has hit the screen so that it is not under- or over-exposed. Under-exposure is when the screen has not been hit with enough light, so when it is washed all of the emulsion runs and you are left back at square one. Over-exposure means too much light has hit the screen. Even if a positive has been placed down, too much light can result in loss of detail and shapes, as the light starts to almost eat around the positives. Over-exposure is much more common in very detailed positives or high-frequency halftones (see page 166).

Step 17 – It's time to hit the go button. First the vacuum engages and it's at this point that you can check that it is really doing its job and everything is nice and flat. If you realize you've made a mistake, or perhaps the vacuum isn't working as efficiently as it could, then stop the machine before the light turns on. As long as the light hasn't turned on, then opening it back up to make changes is fine, but if the light has touched it even for a second then the nature of the emulsion will have changed, and moving your image may result in a bad exposure.

Step 18 – Once the exposure unit has finished, then pop it open and take the screen out. Remember to put the positive somewhere safe as it will be needed later.

TIPS

Make sure that the vacuum is working properly on your exposure unit and is sealed the whole way around. If it's not working properly, then flattening the artwork down can cause small gaps in between the positive and the screen. This means that when the light hits it, a clean line won't be exposed onto the screen because the light will disperse slightly in that tiny gap.

Step 19 – Take the screen through to a wash-out area, trying to avoid contact with light. Parts of the emulsion have now hardened, but parts are still sensitive to light.

Step 20 – Start by covering your screen in water. You might almost immediately be able to see the difference between the hardened emulsion and the emulsion you can wash out of the screen.

Step 21 – Using a sponge, start to scrub over your screen, focusing on the areas where your design is. Flip your screen over and work the sponge over the back as well. You want the mesh where your design is to be completely yellow and open. If you leave any emulsion in there, this will affect your print later down the line.

Don't be afraid to be vigorous with the sponge on the tough areas. It can take a bit of elbow grease.

Step 22 – Have a thorough check over your screen by holding it up to a light source and look for any emulsion remaining in areas it shouldn't.

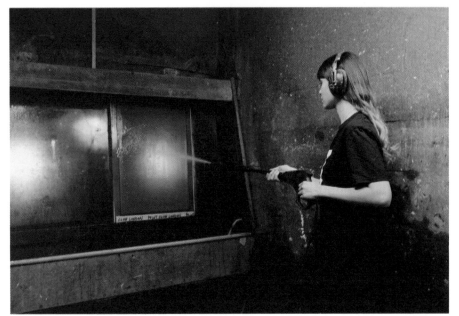

Step 23 – Use a pressure washer to blast away any of the very stubborn bits of emulsion. With older screens emulsion can sometimes be harder to clean out. Be gentle when using the pressure washer. Start with it pointing away from the screen and gently work over the desired areas, while keeping it moving at all times. If you are too aggressive with it, or leave it in one place, then you risk blasting away hardened emulsion, which can then ruin your design. Even though the emulsion has been hardened by the light, it's not invincible – enough pressure will blast it out!

You can now leave your screen to dry. If the weather is good, leave it out in the sun.

Step 24 – Once the screen is dry, it's time to check the stencil for any pin-holes or mistakes. Pin-holes are small gaps in the emulsion that shouldn't be there. If ignored, ink may pass through them when printing, which can ruin a print. Pin-holes occur when dust or hair makes its way onto screens when coating with emulsion. It can then come away along with the emulsion covering it when washing out after exposing. Most pin-holes can be easy to correct, though, so never fear. Also, don't worry about the open mesh around your emulsion at the moment – you can deal with that afterwards. The easiest way to check for pin-holes is by placing your exposed screen over a light box. If you spot any open mesh, apply some emulsion to the screen using a paint brush or a piece of card. Make sure you fill the holes, but don't apply too much.

Step 25 – A paint brush can be used to get rid of any pin-holes that might be contained within your design.

TIPS
You don't want to spoil your container of emulsion by leaving it open in a light room. You can dip a bit of card into it, shut the lid, and use the card as a palette.

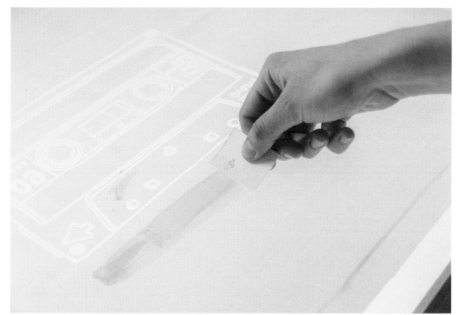

Step 26 – A small bit of cardboard can be used to smear emulsion across large areas containing any pin-holes. By flattening the emulsion out it will keep the drying time down and there won't be any ridges on your mesh. Once you are certain that all the pin-holes have been filled in – take care to look both inside and outside your stencil – then you can allow it to dry. You could place it inside a drying unit again, or speed things up by using a hairdryer.

Step 27 – There is one more step left before the screen is ready to print. The open mesh around the emulsion must be covered up. By covering the pin-holes, the only place ink can pass through your screen is where your design is. Use brown packing tape rather than emulsion at this stage. Tape peels away very easily at the end of the process when water is applied. It should be stuck down securely, so it is half on the mesh and half on the frame. If you do it this way, then no ink will be able to pass through at all. Keep all tape on the top of the screen at this point. Ideally, when printing, you don't want anything to be on the mesh because it could get in the way or add friction.

Step 28 – Make sure you cover all four edges with at least one strip of tape half on the mesh and half on the frame. If there is more open mesh on your screen, just keep laying strips of tape until it overlaps the emulsion.

Remember that the screen must be placed in the exposure unit one more time to harden the emulsion that you've just applied. Use a high exposure value to make sure that it's definitely hardened into your screen.

You should now be left with a completed stencilled screen. If exposed, pin-holed and taped correctly, then your design should come out nice and clean and you will encounter fewer problems when printing.

COLOUR MIXING

Learning how to mix an exact colour in printing
is an art in itself. Here is a method for creating
a Pantone-specific ink colour.

Step 1 – Make sure you have everything you need to hand: the inks
you will need to mix your desired colour, a Pantone swatch book,
various mixing palette knives, cups and some scales. You will also
need some test paper, a test screen and a squeegee.

Step 2 – Make a note of the name of the Pantone colour you
have picked and the colours needed to make it. These will be on
the Pantone swatch. The Pantone matching system has 13 base
pigments (14 including black).

Step 3 – Pour each ink into a different cup. The cups need to be
identical. Try to pour roughly the same amount into each.

Step 4 – Now you have three cups with the colours you need.

Step 5 – Weigh each container and make a note of its weight.

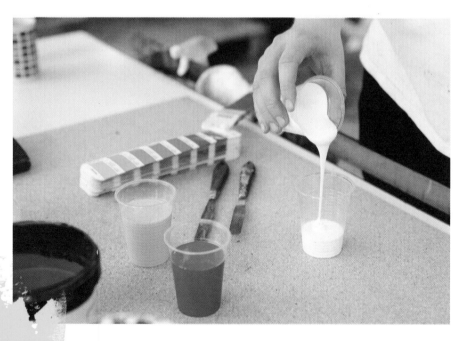

Step 6 – It's time to mix your final colour. At this stage just try to get close to the colour you need by eye. Try to keep your ink containers separate so that the colours don't contaminate each other.

Step 7 – Using a palette knife at this point really helps because it allows a precise amount of ink to be added. Be sure not to spill any when doing this, as you are relying on the weights of the inks to make your final formula.

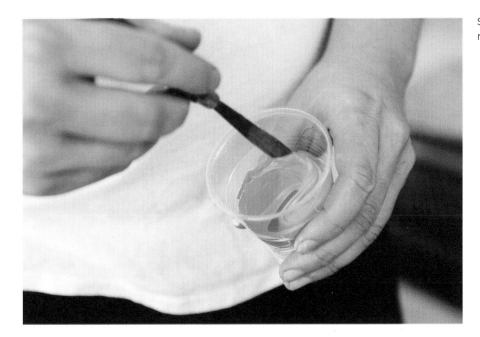

Step 8 – Make sure you mix the inks up really well in your container.

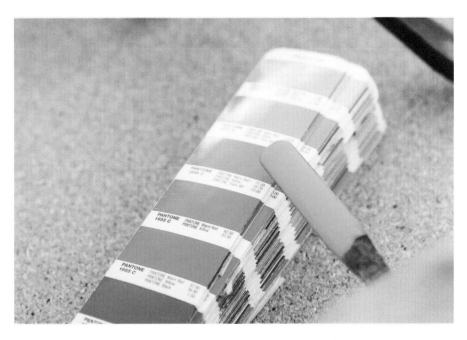

Step 9 – Refer to your Pantone swatch to see if the colour is close. The colour will look slightly different when used for printing so this isn't your final colour.

Step 10 – Use a small screen with a little square exposed to do a test print using your colour. If you have a small screen, you shouldn't need to lock your screen into a bed – instead you can use your hand to hold your frame up, which will create a snap (see the tip on page 76) and allow you to print. Once you've printed, be sure to clean the ink out of your screen.

TIPS

This is a good point to test how your inks sit on top of each other. If your print has an overlay in it, then you need to make sure your inks are transparent enough. To thin them out use a screenprinting binder/medium, but be careful not to use too much. The thinner the ink, the less strong the colour will appear when printed.

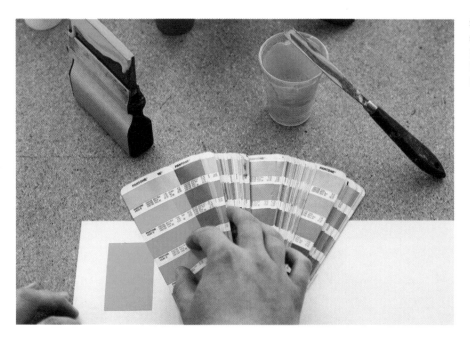

Step 11 – You can now look at your Pantone swatch and see how close your colour is. In this case, the colour is slightly lighter than it needs to be so a bit more red should be added.

Step 12 – The red has been added and another test print has been done. Here, you can see it's still a bit too light, so more red needs to be added.

Step 13 – The colour has been mixed and re-printed two more times, and is now spot on. It can take some time to mix by eye, but be conservative about the amounts added each time. If you use too much of one colour, then it might not be possible to mix up your desired colour with your initial range of inks.

Step 14 – The next step is to measure how much ink remains in each container and make a note of this next to the original weights. Subtract the totals from each other to work out how much of each ink you used from each container.

Step 15 – You can work out the percentage of each ink needed to mix your desired Pantone colour. Calculate the weight of all the ink used, then divide the weight of each ink by the total sum and multiply by 100. This will give you a percentage of how much of each colour to use. Make sure your ratios add up to 100 at the end.

In the future, when you need to mix your ink, simply work out the total weight of the ink you would like to mix, and then calculate the percentages using your formula. Keep a personal swatch of your inks together to avoid having to remix colours.

REGISTRATION AND SCREEN SET UP

Once you've made your screen up and mixed your inks, then you need to set up your screen on a print bed and get your paper registered. Registration is the process of lining up the stencil on your screen so it prints in the right place on your paper. Locking your screen into a bed means it will land and print in one spot only. The guides are needed so you know where to place your paper when printing. Here, the first layer that is going to be printed is the blue. Normally the lightest colour in the piece would be printed first and the darkest last. This is generally because the opacity of darker inks is higher than lighter inks.

TIPS

Once you've registered, try not to change the snap or move the screen. Changing the snap even a bit can result in a small amount of mis-registration, and on a multi-layered print that's not ideal! You can read more about what the snap is on page 79.

Use sturdy bits of card or even small sticky plastic registration markers so they don't degrade during a large print run. If you are printing a lot and using weak or thin paper as registration marks, then they may start to move slightly.

Step 1 – Get a sheet of paper from the supply you will be printing your edition on and any positives you used to expose your screens.

Step 2 – Use masking tape to stick down the positives where you would like to print them on the paper. It's important to stick all the layers down, so that you have a sense of how the whole print will sit on the page.

Step 3 – Once the paper is underneath the screen it can be impossible to move it around, so you need to make some paper handles that you can use to manoeuvre the paper. Cut long strips of paper and attach them to the bottom and side of the paper with small pieces of masking tape. Make sure you place the handles in the centre of the edges for maximum control.

Step 4 – Lock your screen in place so that you know exactly where your stencil will land on the bed when printing. Align your registered print from below, so it sits directly below your stencil.

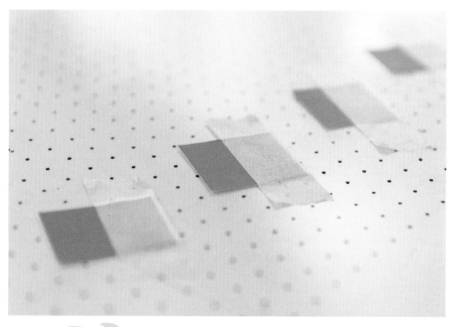

Step 5 – Make four registration markers. These will be stuck onto the bed and will serve as a guide for your paper to slot into when printing. Simply cut down thin strips of paper (make sure they aren't too much thicker or thinner than the paper you are printing on) and stick a strip of masking tape over the end. The tape should be flush with the end of the paper.

Step 6 – With the screen lowered, use the paper handles to move your registered image around until it aligns with your stencil. Note that the mesh does not sit directly on the table, but is hovering just above it. This is called the snap. Use your hand to push the mesh down and eliminate the snap so that your registered image below directly lines up. This stage can be a bit tricky, but it's important to ensure that your prints come out exactly how you want them to.

Step 7 – Once you are sure the print and screen align, then place your registration markers down. Stick two in a bottom corner of your print. Place the tape end against the paper, making sure it is as in line as possible.

Step 8 – Once you have placed the corner registration marks, then place the final two along the same edges but at the other end of the paper.

You only need registration marks down these two sides of your print. As long as there is a solid corner to place your paper into, then registration shouldn't be an issue. If you place registration markers on three sides, you may encounter trouble placing your paper because of the very minor differences in the way paper can be cut. However, any paper discrepancies won't show when registering paper into one corner.

PRINTING PART 1
FLOODING, PULLING AND LOTS OF SCRAP PAPER

TIPS

Make sure you have lots of scrap paper to hand. You don't want to have to run around to find more if you run out. It's always good to keep a supply of personal scrap paper to use, but make sure you have a few cleaner sheets to hand. Before you move onto your good paper, you need to make sure your design is printing properly – you can't check it's coming out well if you are printing onto paper that has other designs already printed onto it.

Depending on your design, you may not want to flood too much ink over your screen. If there are lots of thin lines, it might dry more quickly, so additional ink might be needed. However, flooding too much ink over the screen may result in too much ink being printed out. If you are consistently printing out bleeding artwork, then try using a little less ink.

Make sure you keep the squeegee at a 45-degree angle when going up and down the screen. If the squeegee is too vertical when printing, then too much ink will be forced through the screen and it will bleed.

If your design doesn't print perfectly after a few prints, don't just give up. Check the next section that explains how to fix mistakes while printing. However, it is important that you make sure that your stencil has exposed perfectly compared to your positive. No amount of cleaning will make your design come out properly if your stencil wasn't exposed correctly.

With your image registered and your colours mixed, it's time to start printing at last. The two main parts to printing are 'flooding' and 'pulling'. Flooding fills the stencil up with ink and pulling forces the ink out of the stencil onto the mesh. Most print beds are different from each other, but have the same basic set-up. They will have one or two movable bars to lock your screen into place and a vacuum system. The vacuum is very important when printing as it holds the paper down and in place when the ink hits, which allows for a smooth application.

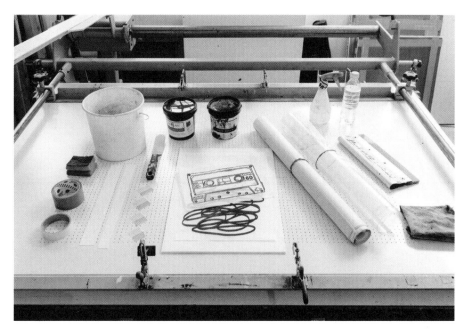

Step 1 – Once the first flood begins, the print process has started. You should make sure that you have everything you need at this point. Check that you have scrap paper, good paper, a good ink supply, a palette knife, a bucket of water and sponge, and some water for yourself to drink. It can be thirsty work.

Step 2 – First you will need a squeegee that's the right size. Ideally you want something that's just a bit bigger, a centimetre or two either side, than your stencil. When printing on paper, you will need to use a hard squeegee (see page 24). When handling a squeegee, try to keep a firm grip at all times. The handle should be in contact with your palm, with no gaps. Your hands should be placed roughly a centimetre or two in from the edges, and be in the same place on either side. If you're handling a squeegee with one hand when you're flooding, then make sure it's right in the middle.

Whenever the squeegee is in contact with the screen, it should be roughly at a 45-degree angle directed towards you.

Step 3 – The snap is the space between your mesh and the bed itself. This should be checked before printing. There needs to be a gap between the mesh and your paper so that when printing only a fine amount of ink hits your paper. It should be adjustable with a screw on the edges of the bed. A squeegee or your hand can be used to measure this gap.

If the snap is too small and your mesh is too close, you may get a blotchy image, as too much ink is being applied. If the snap is too high, then you may not have the strength required to print. The ink in your print will start to dry in and your stencil won't print properly.

Step 4 – Print onto scrap paper to start with. Mistakes can happen and you don't want to waste the paper for your final edition. Once you are sure your prints are coming out how they should, then move onto your good paper. Place a sheet of scrap underneath your screen. If it's a different size to your final, don't worry about registering it up into your guide – just be sure your stencil will hit it.

Step 5 – Hold the frame so that it is well above your paper and pour a big strip of ink along the bottom of your stencil (it should be roughly 5 cm [2 in.] away from it) and make sure you don't get any in the stencil. This line is going to act as your start and end points for now. Turn on the vacuum on the bed. You need to make sure that you do this before printing.

Step 6 – Dip your squeegee right into the ink and give it a wiggle left and right. The aim of this is to wet the blade a little bit, coating the squeegee, so that the first movement over the screen isn't staggered due to dryness.

Step 7 – It's time for the first flood. When flooding make sure that your screen is elevated away from your paper to stop any of the mesh touching it. You can either rest the frame on your stomach and use both hands to flood, or a slightly more advanced technique is to use one hand to hold the frame still and have the other hand on the squeegee.

Place the squeegee beneath the ink, taking as much as you can (while keeping the 45-degree angle mentioned earlier), and gently start to push the ink up the screen and over your stencil. Flooding does not require a lot of strength – the ink just needs to be pushed over the screen so it can sit in your stencil. The first flood sometimes isn't a very smooth motion because the screen is dry, but it will become much easier.

Step 8 – Keep going until you pass your image and stop around a centimetre or two past it. There is no need to keep flooding up to the top of the frame. Remember, the area you are concerned with is your stencil, so you only need to flood and pull just past that. Even an extra couple of centimetres of flooding and printing over a big run of prints can add up to a lot of energy used.

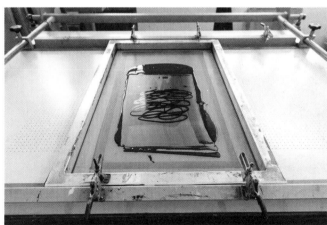

Step 9 – Once you've done your first flood, your screen should look a little like this. Now that the ink is at the top of the screen and your stencil is flooded it's time to pull a print.

Step 10 – Lower the screen down so it's in its resting position on the bed. Position the squeegee above the ink and push down hard. When printing, you need to feel the squeegee touching the bed below it, otherwise you won't be pushing the ink onto the paper. With a firm grip and the same 45-degree angle, pull the squeegee down towards yourself and back to your starting point.

Step 11 – Before lifting the screen up and admiring your print, you need to give the screen another flood, just as you did with the first one. Place the squeegee behind the ink and take it all back to the top again. Once the process has begun, you always need to keep the screen flooded after pulling a print. Even though you have just forced ink out of your stencil, small traces of it will remain and will dry into the screen unless you flood it. Flooding it full of ink will drastically increase the amount of time the ink takes to dry. By continually flooding and printing, hopefully the ink won't dry in at all.

Step 12 – Leave the squeegee against the side of the screen as shown here. This way, when the frame is lifted up, it won't fall over. It also doesn't touch your stencil pushed to the side.

Step 13 – Lift your screen up and there you have it – your first print. Bear in mind that often the first print doesn't look the best. It can take time to get the ink flowing on your screen and it can take a good few pulls on some scrap paper before the prints start looking good.

Step 14 – Take your scrap paper off the bed, place it carefully on a drying rack and put some more paper in.

Step 15 – Keep printing on scrap until you are sure your design is coming out properly. Have a good look at your prints and check for any pin-holes you may have missed that are printing on your paper. Also check for anything that looks wrong. Have your original positive to hand for reference.

PRINTING PART 2
THE GOOD PAPER

Once you are sure your prints are printing out as they should, then it's time to move onto the paper you want to use for your final edition.

TIPS

When registering paper, always try to slot it into your registration marks in the same way. Make sure the corner you slot it into is very firmly stuck to the bed. It takes time to get it right, but it means you are placing the paper correctly each time.

If you are printing a very large edition of prints, it can sometimes be good to clean up halfway through. Ink can start to get tacky when it has been sitting on a screen for a long time, and even if problems with your print aren't immediately visible, there might be some minor changes in the thickness or application of ink onto the paper.

Step 1 – Make sure you have clean hands and then slide your paper into your registration marks.

Step 2 – Be diligent in making sure the paper is firmly pushed into your markers on the table. If it's not, it will be mis-registered when you print. It might not be clear when printing, but if it's a multi-layered print you will notice the mistakes later on.

Step 3 – Keep checking to make sure no more mistakes appear. If they do, move back onto scrap paper and eliminate the mistakes before continuing with your edition paper.

Step 4 – Be gentle when placing your prints onto a drying rack as you don't want to damage them.

PRINTING PART 3
REGISTERING YOUR SECOND LAYER

If you have a multi-layered print, this section will show you how to register a second layer on top of the first. Make sure your first-layer prints are all dry and get your screen locked in as you did the first time round. In this case, a sheet of acetate attached to the bed will be used to register rather than screen registration as before. It's slightly more accurate than using screen registration. There may be changes in the position where your first layer prints are sitting (depending on how careful you were), so you need to have a way of knowing where your prints will land. Once you've begun printing, you can't use through-screen registration as the ink will get everywhere.

TIPS

Make sure the acetate is very firmly fixed to the table with tape. If you are using it to register your image to paper and it's shifting slightly, it will never register properly to your screen.

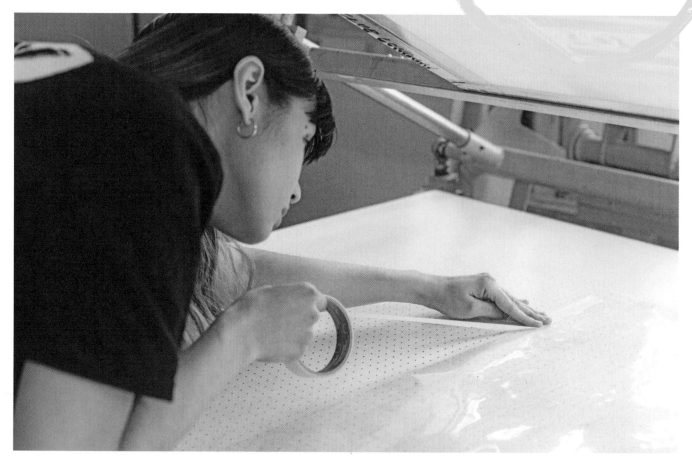

Step 1 – Start by sticking down a flat sheet of acetate onto the bed on one side. You need to make sure that your stencil will land on it, and that you have enough room to manoeuvre your paper below it without it being hindered by the tape.

If you are printing on deckled-edge paper and aren't confident with registration or are simply printing something that is extremely difficult to align, it may be that you need to use the acetate for every print you do. This will take longer as it means constantly flipping the acetate over and registering. It will, however, ensure that every print is spot on.

You may find that when you were printing your first layer there was a slight shift in registration at some point. If all your prints are in order from when you printed before, it may be that when you reach a certain point your second layer of registration starts to miss target. If this consistently happens, it may be worth re-registering the remainder of your prints using the acetate.

It seems obvious, but keep your acetate clean. Don't use a dirty sheet, because it may give you problems when registering something very tight.

Step 2 – Turn the vacuum on and print onto your acetate as normal. Give your screen a flood, but this time registration may take some time so you should do something called a double flood. This is exactly what it sounds like – flooding the screen twice. Once you've flooded as normal, and your ink is at the top of the screen, gently bring it all back down the screen again. By coating ink over your stencil twice, it increases the amount of time that ink could dry into your screen.

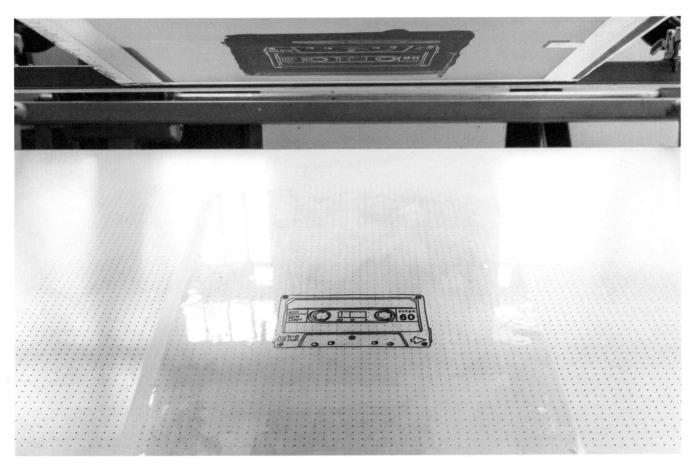

Step 3 – Here is the printed image on the layer of acetate. Now you know exactly where your image is going to land on the bed and you can align your first-layer print to this.

Step 4 – Remember to turn your vacuum off and slide your paper underneath the acetate.

Step 5 – Very carefully align the two layers, making sure that the whole piece is registered properly. Take your time doing this because if you don't do it correctly, you will have to do it again. This is where the extra time of the double flood is going to count.

Step 6 – Carefully peel back the acetate, while keeping a hand on your print so it can't move. Flip it over, but don't peel it off the bed as you may need it again. If there is a lot of ink on the acetate, it may be wet and smudge when you peel it off. You could use a hairdryer to blast it quickly with heat to keep the print bed clean and the image on the acetate crisp.

Step 7 – Just as before, place registration markers down so you know where to put your paper.

Step 8 – If you start printing and then you notice that your images are mis-aligned (see left), then it means that your first layer was printed in different places on your paper.

Step 9 – If this has happened, you can fix it, but this can be very time consuming. First make sure that all of your prints are lining up differently. It may be that by chance the print you used to register was the one that wasn't lining up properly. If they are all different, then you will need to acetate register each new print. This will mean that every print's layers will line up. The first thing to do is to remove your registration markers, as they will hinder your paper moving. Then register a print so it is correct and lay some masking tape down in the place of your registration markers. This will serve as a rough guide to slide your paper into when registering to the acetate and it won't get in the way if you need to move the paper around.

PRINTING PART 4
THE CLEAN UP

You've finished printing, but the work isn't over quite yet. You probably have a very messy screen in front of you and you need to get it clean. To remove the emulsion from the screen use a chemical stencil stripper. This is going to reverse the effects of the light hitting the emulsion, break it down and make it susceptible to water.

TIPS

Don't leave large bits of ink on your screen before using stencil strip. Such ink normally gets stuck down the side of the frame and then will appear when you start scrubbing it. A lot of ink on the screen can just negate the effects of the stencil stripper so be diligent when cleaning beforehand.

When removing ink from the screen, be careful near the edges where the mesh touches the frame. If you aren't paying attention, you may accidentally slide a palette knife too far underneath the frame and rip the mesh.

When cleaning a squeegee, make sure you remove the ink from where the rubber blade meets the handle. There is nothing worse than going to print next time and ink that has been trapped in the gap leaks out. This can ruin prints.

Step 1 – Start by grabbing your container of ink and palette knife to salvage any ink. Remember to salvage any ink on your squeegee as well.

Step 2 – Unlock your screen from the bed and take it to a wash-out room. Get all of the ink off your screen. This can easily be done with water and a sponge. If you have just printed a long run, then some of the ink might be a bit tricky to get off. You can use a pressure washer if it's really stubborn.

Step 3 – Once you've wet the screen, then you can take the tape off. It should just peel away, but if you try to rip it off before wetting the screen, you run the risk of ripping the mesh. Sometimes a bit of ink can remain underneath the tape, so, after it's all off, give the screen one more wash to make sure there's no more ink on it.

Step 4 – To strip the screen and remove the emulsion, start by spraying a healthy dose of stencil stripper on both sides of your screen. Some stencil strip can have hazardous chemicals within it, so you should consult the manufacture about appropriate protection.

Step 5 – Using a bristled brush, repeatedly scrub in circles over your screen. You are trying to remove the emulsion from the mesh, so make sure you scrub all over, especially around the edges where the emulsion might be thicker. Flip the screen over and scrub the back too.

Step 6 – The emulsion should break down the more you scrub but, depending on how old the emulsion or mesh is, this doesn't always happen. Generally, a new screen with new emulsion on it will break down more quickly.

Step 7 – Leave your screen for three to five minutes to allow the stripper to work into the screen. Use the pressure washer to eliminate the emulsion. Gently work your way horizontally along your screen. If you scrubbed hard enough, then the emulsion should blast straight out. Keep working the pressure washer over any stubborn spots and try to get a bit closer.

Step 8 – Once you have pressure washed half of the screen, flip it over so it's upside down. If you blast the lower half of the mesh, sometimes the screen can fall forwards. Also, in a backlit scoop coater it's generally a bit darker lower down, so when you blast the bottom of the screen you might not be able to see any little bits of emulsion stuck in your screen. Remember, you don't need to turn the screen around at all, you only need to blast through one side and that should completely eliminate the emulsion.

Step 9 – Be sure to check your screen thoroughly for any emulsion. If you catch it at this point you can normally blast it out, but if it's left it might become trapped in your screen permanently. Once you're sure it's clean, leave it to dry and store it away ready for next time.

PRINTING MISTAKES

If a mistake happens, which it will, keep a cool head and think logically about the problem. It's important to learn how to tackle problems that could arise and make sure that everything is set up as well as it can be before jumping onto your good paper.

1 – If you notice any little dots of ink on your paper, they may because of pin-holes that you've missed. Some can be fixed, but this can be difficult once the print process has begun. Check your print to see where the ink is coming out and then locate the dot on the underside of the screen. Cover it up with a tiny bit of packing tape stuck to the underside of the screen. If the pin-hole has a lot of space around it a bit of tape will be fine, but if it's located in a tricky spot within your design, then trying to put tape on it may not be possible.

Before washing your screen out, try pulling some prints a few times without flooding. Sometimes ink can be forced out of the screen with sheer strength. This won't always work and water will be needed to clean the ink out, but if it does work it saves you a bit of time.

After cleaning your screen, you may need to give the underside a small wipe, as often water will drip through your stencil and end up underneath the screen. It's much easier to give it a quick wipe rather than keep printing with a screen that has inky water below it.

It's always useful to have a clean rag to hand. Also, make sure that after you've used your sponge you wash it properly or change the water. If you keep washing the screen with a dirty sponge, you are just going to make things more messy.

2 – If the image is patchy, it may be that the ink on your screen is starting to dry in. If it's a very small blockage in your screen, it might be possible to clean that area. However, while you are cleaning one spot the rest of your stencil is drying in. Sometimes it can be best to clean the whole thing.

3 – Pull a print out and don't flood it. The best time to clean the screen is while there isn't much ink in the stencil. You should have a clean sponge and water to hand. Take the sponge and ring it out – you don't want lots of water on your screen at this point. Start with the blocked areas and work the sponge over the screen. You may have to keep cleaning the sponge in the water, but don't stop until you can see the ink has been cleaned out of the stencil.

4 – If there is too much water on your screen, give it a quick wipe with a cloth before going back to printing.

5 – Flood your screen and then carry on printing onto scrap paper. Your prints will look bad at first because there will be quite a bit of water on your screen that you will need to print out. After four or five prints, you should notice the difference and hopefully the image will be cleaner. The water should have cleared any blockages and also lubricated the ink so it flows a bit more smoothly.

If the problem persists, you may want to mix a tiny bit of water into your ink, or a small amount of binder to give it a longer drying time.

6 – If you've tried cleaning your screen and ink keeps consistently drying in, it may be that you aren't pulling hard enough! Try standing on a box to give you some extra height so you can push down a bit harder. Alternatively, you can try lowering the snap slightly to make it easier, although lowering it too much may alter where the print will land, which will mean re-registration.

7 – If you've cleaned your screen and there are still problems, then check the stencil itself. If it wasn't exposed properly, then no matter how much cleaning you do your image won't print properly.

When you're printing you need to learn when to give up, and when to start again. If you can see there is a problem with your stencil, you should go back and expose it properly. If you don't, then it can be a waste of time and money.

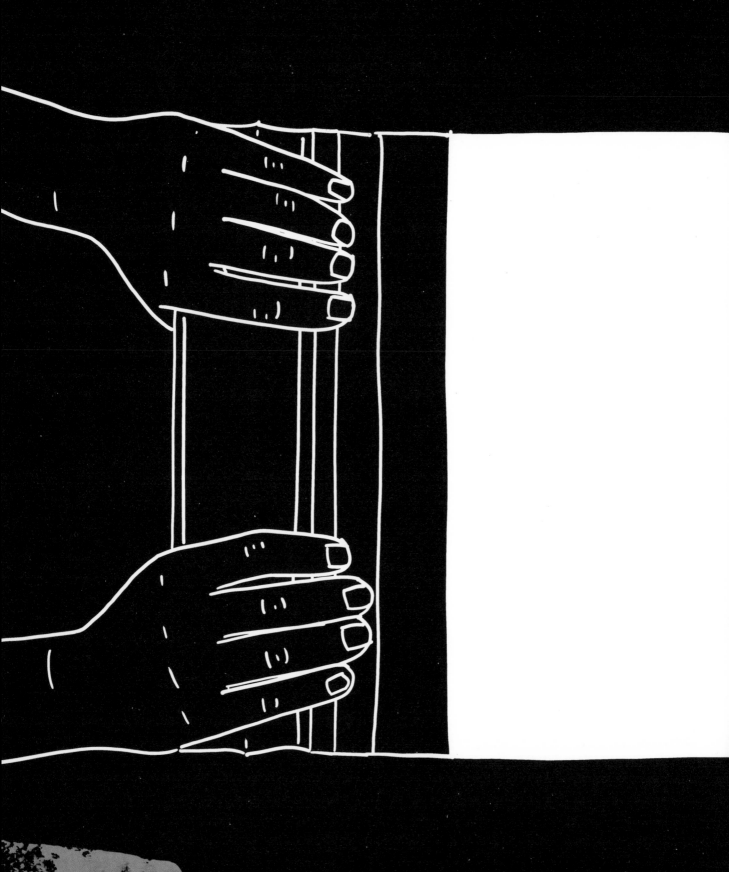

THE BASICS OF PRINTING ON T-SHIRTS

PREPARING YOUR SCREEN
AND REGISTRATION

This section will show you how to set up a T-shirt printing screenprinting press, print a single-layered T-shirt and cure the ink in.

TIPS

When printing on different-sized T-shirts, you may need to register your image a few times, or alternatively dress your platen in a slightly different way each time. For example, if you are printing a design on the pocket area of an extra-small T-shirt and also an extra-large one, the print would need to land in different places on the T-shirt.

Step 1 – The main components of a T-shirt printing screenprinting press are the four printing arms and the platen, the board used to push against when printing the fabric. Screenprinting presses may differ slightly from each other, but they work broadly in the same way.

Step 2 – This is the platen that your garments will be dressed onto. First make sure that you are using one that is the correct size. It's best to have one that snuggly fits your garments, leaving less room for error.

Step 3 – Put your platen in the right position. Bring down the arm you will be using and make sure that it's not making any contact with the platen. If it hits the platen when you bring it down, you will need to move the platen along.

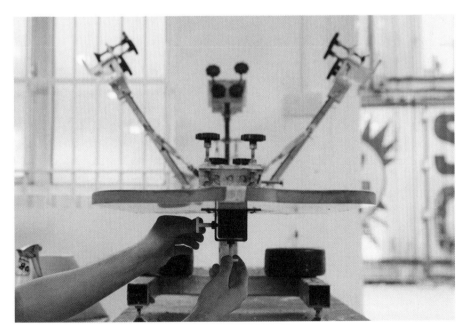

Step 4 – Most platens can be adjusted using the screws located underneath. Once moved, make sure you fix it tightly in place.

Step 5 – Spray a small amount of spray adhesive onto the platen to help keep the garment still.

Step 6 – Now begin by 'dressing' your platen with the T-shirt you will be printing on. The T-shirt must be placed straight onto the platen, so that it can be repeated again and again accurately. Dressing it straight every time can be tricky and is something that you will get better and better at naturally. Using a platen that is a similar width to the T-shirt can help, as it leaves less room for movement.

Step 7 – Make sure that the label of the T-shirt is centred below the platen.

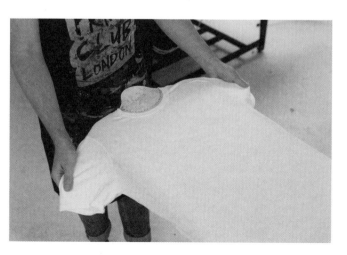

Step 8 – Check that each of the armpits is parallel and equidistant from the platen.

Step 9 – Once you're sure that the garment has been dressed correctly onto the platen, position the artwork. The aim is to centre the artwork onto the platen and make sure it's straight. Artwork is generally placed three or four fingers below the collar line. A ruler can be used to ensure that it's equidistant from the sides. Take a note of the placement of the artwork, as you will need to repeat this process again.

Step 10 – Stick down the artwork with masking tape to make sure it doesn't move about.

Step 11 – Lock your screen into one of the arms. Start by placing it centrally over the platen.

Step 12 – Make sure the screen is locked into place by securing the bolts at the end of the arm.

Step 13 – Bring the screen down over the T-shirt and registered artwork. Measure the position of the positive's alignment on the screen. You should expose the image in this exact place. Measure where it sits on the screen. Remove the screen from the clamp and coat it up (see page 60).

Step 14 – Once your screen is dry, take it to the exposure unit (see pages 59 and 60 for tips) and place your screen on top of your positive in the same way. Make sure that the positive is aligned correctly using the measurements you just made. Once you are sure the screen and positive are in the right place, then expose the screen (see page 60 onwards for tips). Then wash out, pin-hole and tape it up.

Step 15 – Re-dress your platen and re-attach your artwork to your T-shirt as you did before. Loosely attach your screen back into the screenprinting press arm in the same central position as before.

Step 16 – Once the screen is brought down, it should roughly align with your registered image. If it doesn't, then gently adjust the screen until the registered image and your stencil align.

Step 17 – Once the screen has been registered, you should very firmly clamp it in so that it won't move.

Step 18 – If your screenprinting press has a guiding bolt to tighten it up, make sure that the arm doesn't have too much give when you bring it down. You are ready to print.

PRINTING YOUR T·SHIRT

(see page 102)

TIPS

Really do take care when dressing the platen. If you carelessly dress it incorrectly, then you'll ruin the print and the garment.

Pay attention to the spray adhesive. Keep checking the platen to make sure there's enough adhesive to allow the fabric to stick to it.

Be careful when lowering the screen onto the platen. If you notice any creases in the fabric, for example, or can see it's not dressed properly, then redo it.

If your screenprinting press has micro-registration built into it, which is generally a screw going through horizontally where the arm is lowered, make sure it's tight and not loose. If it's loose it will allow the arm to move left and right while printing and could offset your print each time. With the screw tightened up, it should make the arm lower in the same place each time.

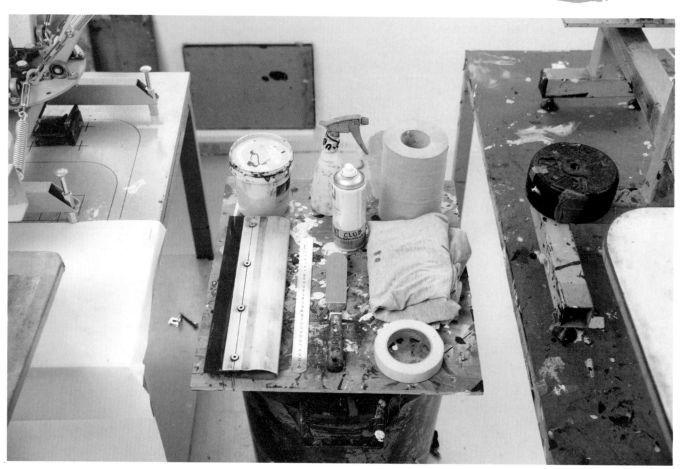

Once you have prepared your screen and registration (see page 102), then you will be ready to print your T-shirt.

Step 1 – Gather all of the materials you might need to hand. One of the things you will need is a spray adhesive, which you will have to use occasionally to keep the platen slightly sticky. When you are printing a T-shirt you don't have a snap, so often the material needs to be secured to the platen – otherwise it could stick to the screen after printing.

Step 2 – Spray your platen with a bit of spray adhesive and start with a rough piece of fabric or an old T-shirt. Clothes can be expensive to print onto, so make sure the ink is flowing through your screen properly before you print onto a T-shirt.

Step 3 – The basics of printing at this point are very similar to printing on paper. For a slightly more detailed instruction of flooding and printing see page 80. Put a healthy dose of ink along the bottom of your screen, but make sure it doesn't go onto any of the stencil to start with.

Step 4 – Keep the screen raised above your garment and gently flood your stencil with ink. You don't need to flood the entire screen, just push the ink up to a centimetre or two above your design.

Step 5 – Carefully lower your screen onto your garment. Because there isn't a snap with fabric-printing it means that as soon as the screen is lowered the flooded stencil will have made contact with the garment. Place your squeegee behind the ink left at the top of the screen, ready to print it out.

Step 6 – Firmly bring your squeegee down over your stencil, pushing all of the ink through onto your garment.

Step 7 – Once printed, carefully lift the screen off the garment and give it a flood to keep ink in your stencil so it doesn't dry up.

Step 8 – Once you're happy with how your prints are looking, then start printing onto your good garments. If you are having problems printing, check out the printing mistakes section before moving on.

Step 9 – When you're using your rough materials and removing the T-shirt from the platen, you don't have to take much care, but you will have to be very careful with your good clothes. If you accidentally fold the material onto itself, then it's going to ruin the design. Once printed, start by pinching the shoulders and peeling the T-shirt off the platen. This may take a bit of effort, depending on how much spray adhesive you've used.

Step 10 – Keep a good hold of the shoulders and take your time to pull the T-shirt off the platen. The next step is to dry your T-shirt. Check the next section for tips on how to do this.

CURING YOUR T-SHIRT

TIPS

Check the speed setting on your conveyor dryer. If you are having problems with ink washing out of the fabric, it may be that it's running through the heat too fast.

If printing on thicker materials, such as a hoody for example, be sure to make it lie as flat as possible when running it through the tunnel. The more raised off the conveyor belt, the closer it is to the heating element and if it's too high then it could burn.

If printing white on black, be sure to run through a conveyor dryer multiple times. Lighter colours on darker fabrics tend not to stay on as well due to the pigment.

Water-based fabric ink is specifically designed to bond to the material so it ensures a wash-fast print when heated to a specific temperature for a specific time. Different inks will cure at different temperatures. It may be worth contacting the manufacturer of the brand you are using to be sure.

Step 1 – If you have a conveyor dryer, as Print Club does, then make sure it's ready to be used. This one operates at 400°F (204°C) and has a built-in conveyor belt to pass the material through the heat and out the other side safely.

Step 2 – Once you've printed your T-shirt, bring it over to the conveyor dryer while holding it by the shoulders. Make sure the fabric doesn't fold over onto itself and potentially ruin your garment.

Step 3 – Lay the T-shirt on the conveyor belt and let it roll through the machine. Make sure it is flat so that all of the ink is exposed to the heat.

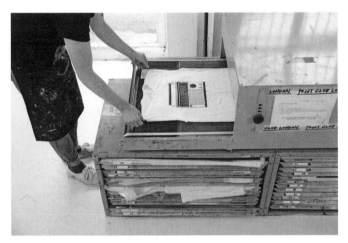

Step 4 – Some tunnels may have heating elements on the side, so it can be useful to fold the sleeves in so they aren't too close to the heat. Multiple passes through the tunnel can help to ensure that the ink is cured in properly. Also, with a large run of T-shirts it is best to do a test wash to make sure the ink is cured in.

Step 5 – Not every studio is equipped with a conveyor dryer, but a heat gun and domestic iron can also be used to cure the ink in. Once you've printed your garment, blast it with a heat gun to make sure it's dry. Then you can place it down and print the rest of your fabric. Once you've finished printing, iron the print with a dry iron turned up to the hottest setting.

PRINTING MISTAKES

Here are a few common problems you may encounter when printing onto a T-shirt.

TIPS

As the mesh count is much lower than a paper screen, occasionally bits of emulsion can come off the screen while printing and leave little holes where ink can come through. Have some brown tape to hand to be able to cover up any such holes or, alternatively, tippex can be used on the screen. It washes straight off with water when you are done.

Experiment with different squeegee types. If you are having trouble forcing ink onto your fabric, you could use a curved-blade squeegee rather than a D-cut one. The curve of the blade pushes more ink through the screen, which helps force the ink into the fabric.

Make sure that your designs are coming out well before moving onto your fabric or garments, especially after washing your screen. You really don't want to waste your fabric.

1 – If your print is coming out oversaturated, then you may be using a bit too much ink. Try using less ink when flooding and printing.

2 – Remember to print onto an old bit of material first to make sure you aren't wasting your good garments.

3 – If your design isn't coming through properly, the ink may have dried into the screen. Try adding a bit more ink to your screen and push really hard when printing. Sometimes dry ink can be forced out of your screen with force. If it still looks the same, it means you need to wash your screen.

4 – Remove any ink from the screen using a palette knife.

5 – Spray a generous amount of water onto the screen.

The Basics of Printing on T-shirts

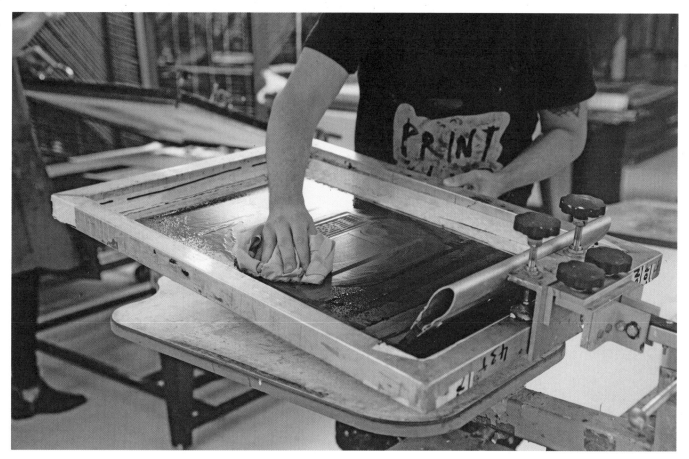

6 – Use a rag or blue roll to wipe the screen gently until you can see the ink being removed from your stencil.

7 – Use a dry cloth or paper towel to wipe the underside of the screen to clean up any water that may have dripped through your stencil. Remember to print onto spare material before moving back, onto your good clothes, as there will most likely be excess water on your screen that you will need to print out.

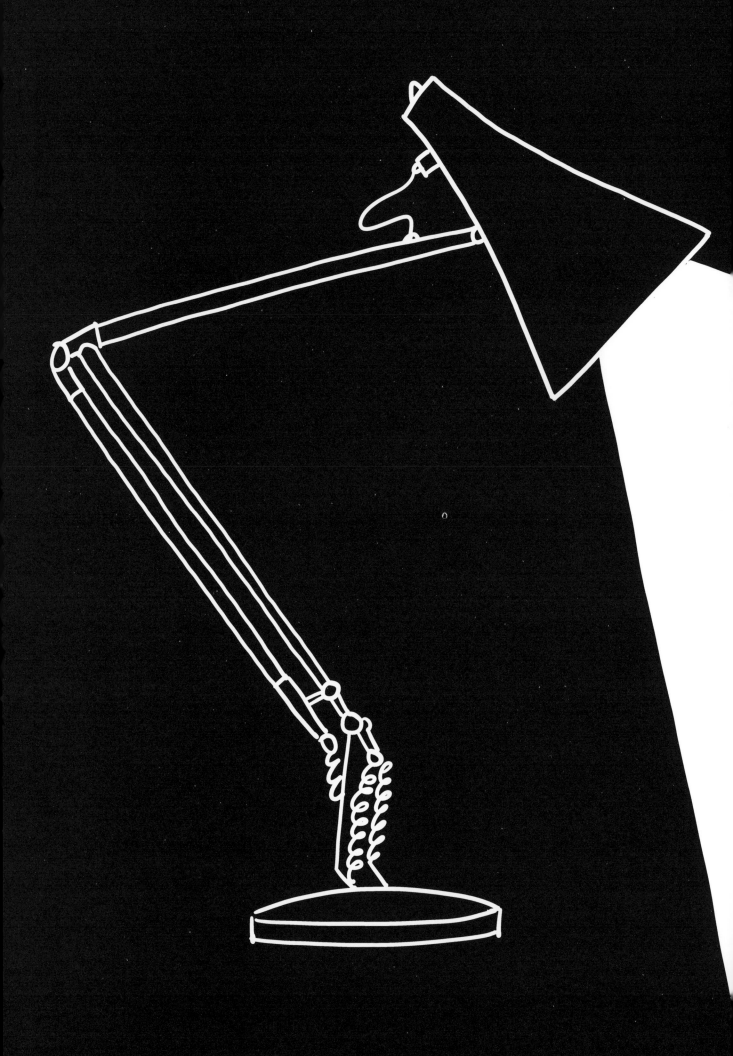

ARTIST SPOTLIGHT

AUGUSTINE AND BRIDGLAND

MONOPRINTING

The duo Danny Augustine and Adam Bridgland are leading printmakers and artists. They graduated from the Royal College of Art in London and collaborated for the first time with a sell-out exhibition, *Flowers For Your Darlings*, at Jealous Gallery, London in 2014. The show was a collection of large monoprint works exploring themes of lust and love, created by painting directly onto the screenprint mesh before printing. The project evolved very organically, almost by accident, developing from an initial interest in combining imagery and text in their respective solo art practices.

'Another method to work with screenprinting is to paint directly onto the mesh before printing with your squeegee. Creating a unique, one-off image onto the surface below is called a monoprint. We used this method in our practice. The result is a very flat surface typical of the screenprint medium, but one that holds a wealth of texture and movement due to the marks made working directly with the ink and screen. The method must be performed quickly to avoid any inks drying into the screen mesh. This speed only adds to the excitement and vibrancy in the work. The process is great to lose any inhibitions and just have fun with expressive marks.'

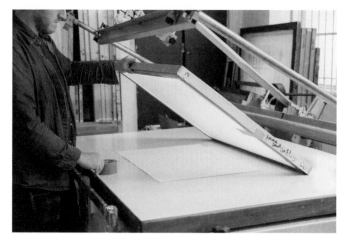

Step 1 – Start with an empty screen and a sheet of paper that you want to print on. There aren't any test prints with monoprinting.

Step 2 – Mask off the area of the screen you won't be printing through using packing tape. This could be any shape you want, but for beginners it's easiest to try a square or a rectangle.

Step 3 – Register this shape to the paper below before painting onto the screen. Make sure that you leave this sheet underneath the screen before painting. Keep the screen flat, since the ink can run, and keep the paper under there ready to print straight onto.

Step 4 – Once the process begins, you will need to move fast, so have all of your brushes and inks to hand.

Step 5 – Start applying your inks to your screen using a soft paint brush.

Step 6 – Keep speedily painting to build up your image.

Step 7 – Apply some clear printing base to any areas that are not covered with ink; this minimizes any streaking and contamination of inks with each other.

Step 8 – Once you are happy with your image, then you will need to place binder on the screen along the length of the squeegee. This allows for the print to be pulled more smoothly. You are now ready to print. Flooding isn't necessary – just grab your squeegee and pull. Augustine and Bridgland decided to use an arm attached to a bed.

Step 9 – A unique one-off monoprint is made. The screen will need to be cleaned quickly as the ink could dry in and damage the mesh.

BEN EINE

STENCIL

Ben Eine is a leading graffiti artist. Born and based in London, he has been working on the scene for over 25 years and has developed an extremely recognizable typographic portfolio. His work is mostly seen in the East End of London.

In 2010 David Cameron gave Barack Obama *Twenty First Century City* by Eine.

His work is currently held in the permanent collections of several galleries worldwide, including the Victoria & Albert Museum, London, and the Museum of Contemporary Art, Los Angeles.

'A spray can has become the tool of my trade, notoriety and income, so it's fitting to make my screenprinting positives using a sprayed stencil. Screenprinting has always been a logical medium for street artists, pulling ink through a screen is very similar in concept to spray painting, just the equipment and environment differ.

Making a positive by hand without a computer is more true to the work I produce on a daily basis. Although the prints I create are the same lettering I've used for some of my most well-known work (designs sprayed onto shop front shutters), they become more than a re-creation and pieces in their own right, because I'm hand creating the positives.'

Step 1 – Here, Eine started by creating his own design that he wanted to stencil and print out onto a blank sheet of paper. The print needs to be the same size as the final print as the positives for exposing will be made from this stencil. Eine has used a fitting P for Print Club (taken from his famous 'Cast Iron' typeface) as the base for his stencil. Next the design needs to be fixed securely onto stencil paper. This provides a durable and precise stencil to work with when cutting and spraying.

Step 2 – Then it's time to start cutting. It's very important to have a think about the order of your colours in terms of printing the final image (see page 137). Here, Eine is starting with the red background to form the top of the P.

Step 3 – One sheet of acetate or tracing paper is needed for each different layer of the print. Once the first part of the stencil has been cut and removed, a sheet of acetate needs to be slid underneath it.

Step 4 – Now it's time to spray black paint through the stencil onto the acetate to form the first layer of your print. The stencil paper needs to be flat against the acetate to get a nice clean edge when spraying.

Step 5 – Here is the first positive ready to be exposed onto a screen, but for the time being this should be put to one side as there is more to do.

Step 6 – This process is primarily used to make original artwork as well as positives, so it's a good idea to make both at the same time. Sliding a good sheet of paper underneath the stencil means you can spray through it onto the paper below. For his piece, Eine has sprayed and created an original alongside the positives and the colours of this piece will be used as a base for the screenprint inks.

Step 7 – The way Eine works is to re-attach the original cut-out piece back into the stencil paper and work more on this to create layered artwork. It requires a bit of forward thinking, but it's a technique he has worked with and perfected over the years.

Step 8 – Black has to be sprayed onto acetate each time. This has to be done slowly. It can be a bit tricky to make things perfect at this stage, but it will be worth it in the end. Once each positive layer has been made, the original has to go back under the stencil so that a new colour can go down.

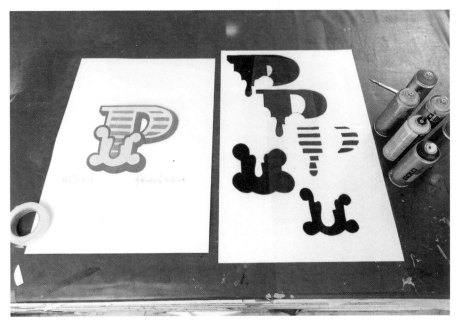

Step 9 – Once all of the layers are completed, you should be left with something similar to this, a selection of black positives each on their own sheet and then a completed spray-painted original. The positives are ready to be exposed as they are and the original is ready to be adorned on someone's wall! Now it's time to prep and print.

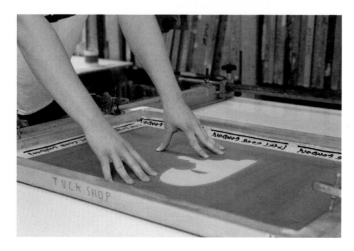

Step 10 – Here, the printer is registering the first layer of the print to the paper.

Step 11 – The first colour going down is red.

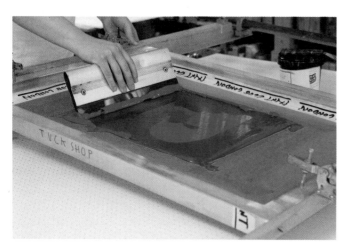

Step 12 – The screen is flooded.

Step 13 – After ensuring that the ink is coming through the stencil well onto scrap paper, the first layer is printed onto the paper from the final edition.

Step 14 – A layer of white has been printed through the yellow layer stencil first because the positives were made from hand-cut stencils. This means the yellow will be nice and punchy when it gets printed.

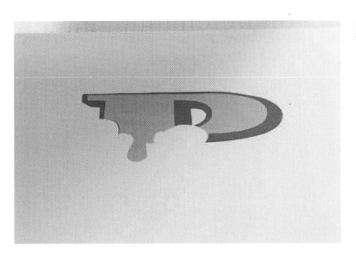

Step 15 – Next is the yellow layer, which has been printed on top of the white.

Step 16 – Here is the fourth layer being printing. The stencils have been exposed side by side on the screen to save time.

Step 17 – Two more layers have been printed and we are left with the final piece.

BEN RIDER
HAND-MADE POSITIVES

Ben Rider is a London-based printmaker, commercial illustrator and teacher. He specializes in making vibrant, edgy work with a punky look and feel.

Rider loves the gratifying nature of print and what it can add to an illustration. To him the sense of physically making something with your hands has an honesty and gives the work a certain soul and character, which challenges the increasingly homogenized slick corporate world.

'I am a fluorescent-ink obsessed illustrator who loves to make massively vibrant work with a raw punky look and feel bursting with energy and loud graphics. My work is influenced a lot by the process of printmaking and the potential it offers to take a really experimental playful approach to the physical producing of the imagery and what this can add to a piece of work.

I love the patina of the process, especially the happy accidents such as offsets, drips, tears and dirty photocopied positives, which to me give the work a certain soul and character.'

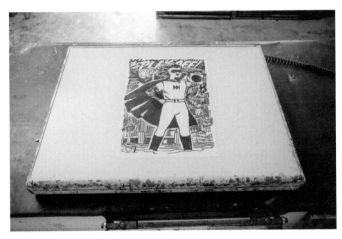

Step 1 – This print consists of a variety of hand-made positives – colour layers that sit underneath a digitally composed layer, which will be printed in black. The black layer has been printed out and will be used as a base to create the positives.

Step 2 – The first technique Rider uses is ripping up and rearranging found type positives. Ripping creates a rough raw texture around the edge. Rider has ripped two type pieces at once so that the pieces are easier to slot together when repositioning.

Step 3 – The positives are rearranged using the black positive layer as a base to make sure they all fit together. A few of the pieces have been scrunched up and, where Rider thought it was necessary, he has cut into them to remove the ink and create a more rugged texture in the positives.

Step 4 – Once he was happy with the composition, Rider used transparent (it's important not to block out the light when exposing) sellotape to stick his positives back together. They can still be moved around later.

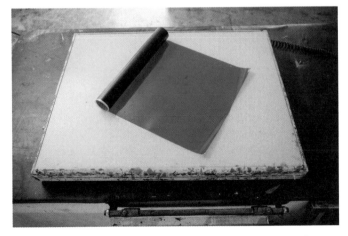

Step 5 – Rubylith is another process that can be used to create a positive. It is a coloured masking film that blocks UV light, as a positive digitally printed out in black would. Rubylith is transparent so you can see through the film, which makes it easier to cut a design in exactly the correct position and scale to the final artwork.

Step 6 – The rubylith is stuck down on top of the artwork. Rider has put his black layer underneath. If both the rubylith and the positive are secure, then the resulting layer will be accurate and precise.

Step 7 – Once in position, Rider uses a sharp knife to cut gently around the areas he wants to colour in his print.

Step 8 – He carefully starts to peel away the rubylith from its acetate sheet.

Step 9 – Great care must be taken when peeling around the shapes.

Step 10 – Here is the rubylith layer with the black positive layer removed from below. This is now ready to go into the exposure unit to be exposed onto a screen as normal.

Step 11 – For the final layers, Rider is using black indian ink (which is very effective at blocking out UV light) to paint directly onto tracing paper placed over the top of the black layer. The tracing paper is firmly taped on top of the layer below to keep everything lined up while painting.

Step 12 – Different textures can be achieved by using different brushes. Here, Rider is using a very rough, big brush to give his shapes a gnarly edge.

Step 13 – This process encourages spontaneous and uncontrolled mark marking. Rider has put large drips of ink on the tracing paper and manipulated the paper so they run down the positive. Remember to do something similar to this after the precise elements have been painted, so you won't need to re-align it to the black layer below.

Step 14 – For one final layer Rider is drawing some little details onto a new sheet of tracing paper stuck over the original black layer. Use an opaque pen rather than one that is solvent-based as it will tend not to block out UV light properly. If you make any mistakes at this point, you can always cut them out and stick a new bit of tracing paper on to redraw.

Step 15 – Here are Rider's positives made using manual techniques alongside his original black layer digital print out. These are all ready to expose as normal.

Step 16 – The first colour has been put down.

Step 17 – Pulling the first layer.

Step 18 – The second yellow layer is being applied.

Step 19 – The first two layers have been printed.

Step 20 – Next is the blue.

Step 21 – Then the green, the last colour before the black.

Step 22 – Here are all of the coloured layers printed, although it looks a bit messy at the moment.

Step 23 – Just one more layer to go.

Step 24 – And here it is. The black pulls everything together to make the final print.

CASSANDRA YAP
GOLD FOILING

Cassandra Yap, originally from Singapore, is an artist and art director based in London. Her work often explores the juxtaposition between dark and beautiful subjects to create the surreal. Her love of pin-ups, the female form and an unhealthy obsession with vintage erotica informs her photomontage halftone-style images that are dark, bold and humorous with a kinky edge.

Her work has been shown at many exhibitions including several *Blisters* shows and at a pop-up gallery at the 3939 Shop at Bluebird, London. She had a solo show at Lay Low Gallery in Palma de Mallorca and was part of a group show, *Revolution*, at Wall Street Gallery in Los Angeles.

'I usually start off mucking about in Photoshop on the Mac, re-imagining found vintage photos into modern works of art. Then I love getting more hands on, screenprinting to actually produce the artwork itself. It's the best of both worlds, so I'm a very lucky gal. I'm especially drawn to foiling, diamond dust and gold leaf – anything that makes the piece a bit different and unique. That said, gold leaf is a right little so and so that requires a steady hand and a very light touch, but I love a challenge (although sometimes it ends up being a very expensive mistake). The hand-finished quality of the gold leaf lifts the print, giving it another dimension as well as a beautiful, ethereal edge, especially when it catches the light.'

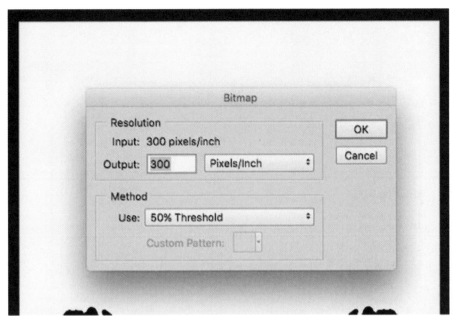

Step 1 – Starting with your design you will need to identify which parts are going to be gold leafed. Here, Yap will be gold leafing the butterfly wings and then printing details on top of them. Prepare the rest of your image as you would normally in Photoshop (see page 48). For the gold-leaf layer we are going to treat it as a flat spot colour, so you need to separate it from the main image and make sure it's pure black by BITMAPPING it.

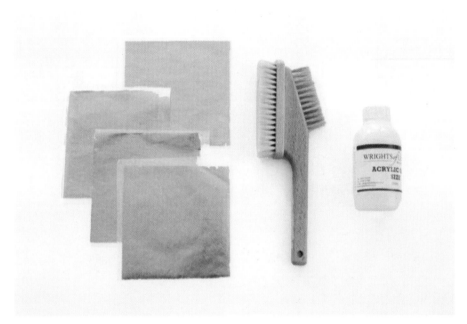

Step 2 – Prepare your screens as normal and get all your materials ready. Sometimes it's good to have a friend with you for the gold leafing, so grab one if available and willing.

Step 3 – The first step is to print a layer of glue through your screen onto the paper. A tricky part of printing with glue is that it is transparent, so ensuring that the design is coming out clean can be a bit hard. To help with this you can mix in a tiny bit of ink to make it visible on the paper.

Step 4 – The glue must be left to dry slightly until it is tacky to the touch. With larger coverage this will take longer so put the kettle on.

Step 5 – Now it's time to get the gold leaf out! Gently start by laying it over the glue areas and smoothing it out so that it's nice and flat. Gold leaf itself tends to come in small quantities so covering a large area can take some time, especially on a big run.

Step 6 – The excess gold leaf needs to be brushed away from the design using a soft-bristled brush. Once the gold leaf has been pushed into the glue, it should be fairly firmly attached to the paper, so don't worry about being too soft with the brush.

Step 7 – Yap has chosen to use gold leaf and then print over the top of it. However, many artists also use gold leaf at the end on top of the ink as a finishing touch. If you are printing on top, make sure the gold leaf is nice and smooth for best results.

Step 8 – Using the gold leaf layer to register, the rest of the design can now be printed on top of it. Here, the blue has been printed and the red layer is aligned up against the wings.

Step 9 – The red layer is printed on top of the blue layer and the gold leaf.

Step 10 – A red layer has been printed and now it's time for the final black layer to go down.

Step 11 – Here is the final layer of black printed.

KATE GIBB

COLLAGE

Kate Gibb has worked as printmaker and illustrator for over
15 years. She is based in a makeshift print studio in Paddington,
London. A silk-screen obsessive, she originally studied printed
textiles. Her inherent love of colour and pattern continually
provides the basis for the majority of her work. She is inspired
by the kind of printing that relies on chance, hiccups and
happy accidents.

'I love using cut-out collage work to make positives as it
allows for spontaneous little accidents. It's also not permanent
– if a mistake is made, another shape can easily be redrawn
and re-cut!'

Step 1 – Before she started, Gibb gathered all the materials she was going to need, including a light box, and printed out a photographic positive she would use as a base for her design, along with another version printed on regular paper to make notes on.

Step 2 – Old photos provided the inspiration for the colours and composition of the shapes.

Step 3 – It is helpful to be able to make notes and draw on a print out of the photograph. If collaging, you may not have a base piece to work around like this.

Step 4 – Using the drawings and notes, Gibb made a rough digital mock-up. As the block colours will be cut out manually, it is useful at this stage to have a visual aid to stick to, although as an organic process this doesn't have to serve as a strict guide.

Step 5 – Gibb placed a large sheet of paper over the top of the base positive on a light box.

Step 6 – Desired block areas are drawn onto the paper and marked with the colour that they will be. In this case, a white layer is going to be printed.

Step 7 – Once the elements were drawn, they were carefully cut out using a scalpel and put to one side. Later on these will be stuck down onto a large sheet of acetate in the correct position to form the positive.

Step 8 – The other shapes were cut out to form the rest of the layers.

Step 9 – The printer then re-assembled the cut-outs and stuck them onto a sheet of acetate using clear tape. When the paper is exposed it will block out the UV light but the tape will allow the light to pass through it.

Step 10 – The printing process began with the white layer going down first.

Step 11 – Next is the yellow.

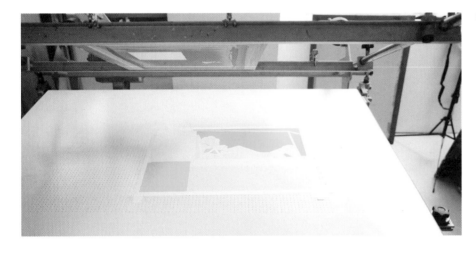

Step 12 – Then the pink.

Step 13 – The final navy layer is being registered.

Step 14 – The final print.

MATTHEW GREEN

HALFTONE

Matthew Green produces beautifully hand-drawn illustrations. His signature style is often compared to wood-cut prints and etchings, but beyond this craftsmanship, and at the heart of all of Green's work, lies an enormous sense of fun. He creates worlds and moments where fantasy can meet the most mundane, from a voyeuristic zebra who resides in an old wooden shed to a glamorous blue tit dining for one.

'The woodland scene I have created focuses on the use of light. I wanted to create a sense of depth and drama to the piece. By applying varying halftones, bigger dots in the foreground and smaller dots towards the woodland opening, I have been able to create an illusion of dark to light while using just black ink.'

Step 1 – Green started with a rough digital version of what the final image will look like. Many shades of grey have been used, since one of the layers of the print will utilize the halftone technique.

Step 2 – Green creates the intricate line drawing that will make up the image. It will be spot colour and not halftoned. The drawing needs to be a scale of the printed artwork – in this case it is a 50 x 70cm 400dpi image.

Step 3 – The image is drawn in pure black, which will make it easier when BITMAPPING later on in the process.

Step 4 – A new layer is made and placed below the line layer. This is the layer that all of the greys will be drawn on. It is important to keep the pure black layer and grey layers separate.

Step 5 – All of the grey shades are now finished. They have been kept on the same layer below the black line work layer. Another halftone layer, which isn't black, will be made on a separate layer.

Step 6 – The grey layer has been copied into a new greyscale document, with the same dimensions.

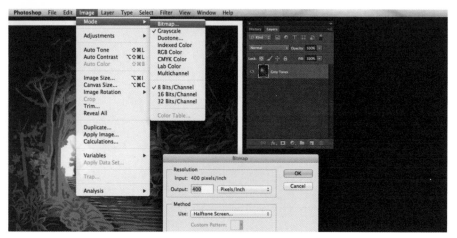

Step 7 – It's now time to HALFTONE the grey layer. There are lots of options with halftone, including the frequency of shapes it will create, the angle they will appear at and the actual shape of them. In this case, Green has chosen a frequency and angle of 45 degrees and round shapes. Forty-five is a good, high frequency and will create very small dots, giving a better illusion of gradient of tone on the eyes. Sometimes using a number that ends in a 5 or 0 can result in a slightly warped visual effect called a moire effect. In this case, it works fine but if you notice an odd pattern appearing in your positives, it may be worth changing the angle of the halftone to something that doesn't end in 0 or 5.

Step 8 – A closer inspection of the halftone will show whether the level of detail desired has been achieved.

TIPS

HALFTONE is a technique used to create the illusion of texture and tone on a positive ready for exposing. Positives are binary in that they will either expose or not onto your screen, so getting various tones on one layer is technically impossible. The HALFTONE process will turn all the information on screen into lots of small pure-black shapes that can vary in size and frequency and give the impression of a change in tone, despite all of the shapes being pure black.

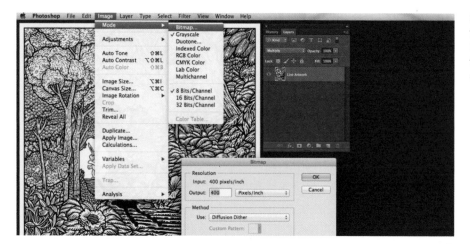

Step 9 – The original line-work layer needs to be BITMAPPED to ensure it is pure black. It has been placed into a new document, to the same dimensions, and BITMAPPED using diffusion dither.

Step 10 – BITMAPPED images must be converted back into greyscale mode to be moved or copied out of a document. The two layers that were bitmapped must now be placed into a document together (they form one layer of the final artwork). It is very important to make sure they are aligned properly.

Step 11 – Both layers are then finally BITMAPPED one more time to merge them together and form one layer that is ready to be printed as a positive.

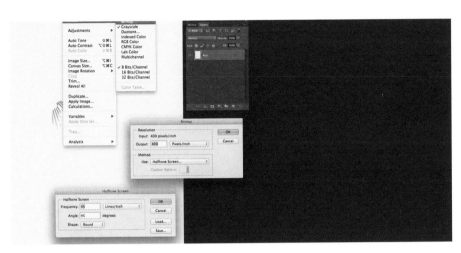

Step 12 – Finally, the second layer must also be HALFTONED. A new document has been made and the layer has been HALFTONED using the same settings as before. Both layers are now ready to be made into positives and printed.

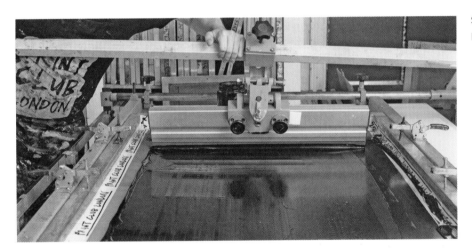

Step 13 – Here is Green's piece being printed. The black layer goes down first.

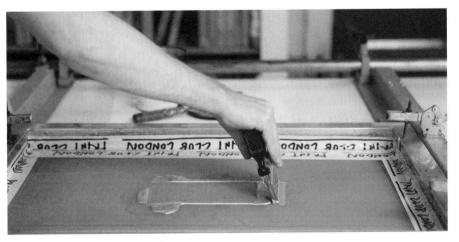

Step 14 – And finally the gold layer.

M.O.L.
COLOUR BLEND

Fred Higginson, who also works under the name of M.O.L. (Ministry of Love), graduated from the Norwich School of Art and Design. He set up his first artist studios in an old church, providing affordable workspace for local artists. Two years later he returned to London and set up more studios, followed a year later by Print Club. As well as having a key role at Print Club, he produces silk screenprints and also sculptures. Higginson's techniques are as eclectic as his influences – he works across various media and uses materials that range from play-doh to the pencil.

'I have always incorporated colour blends in my artwork, I like the unpredictability to them, and they are almost impossible to control so that each print is unique. I have developed a method of printing one colour blend layer and then rotating the screen so that when the second layer is applied it creates an array of colours. I have made a print that will show you how to get the most out of a two-layer colour blend. Alternatively, have a go and see what happens – have fun with a blend.'

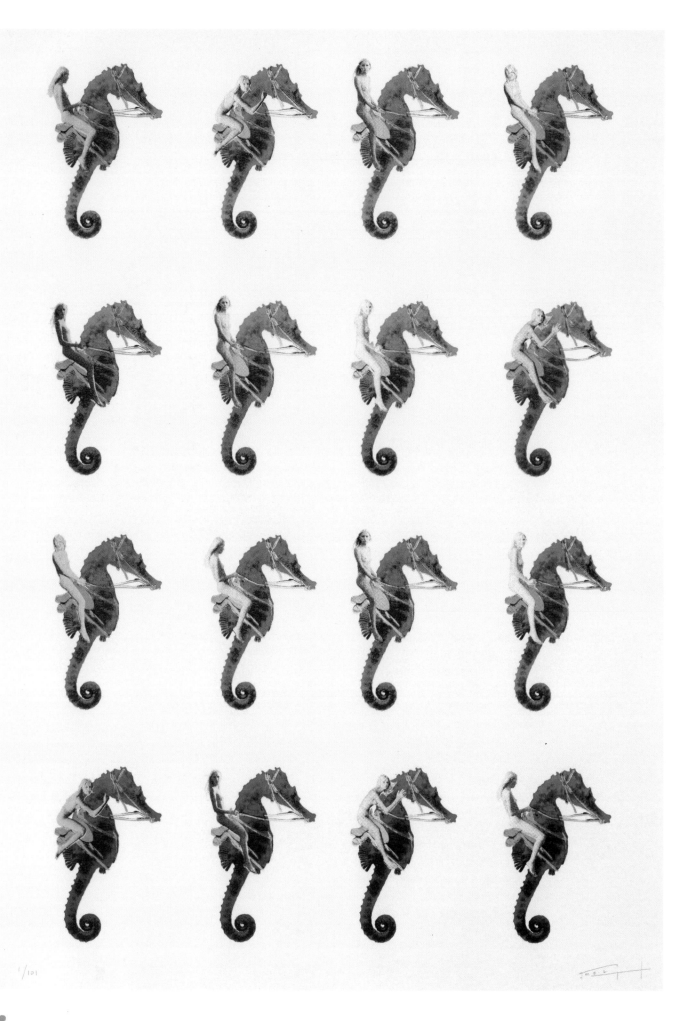

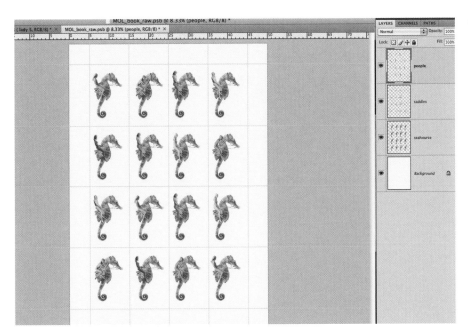

Step 1 – M.O.L. did two blends to create the seahorses and then a final halftone detail layer over the top to finish it off.

Step 2 – The rest of the image is prepared as it would normally be in Photoshop (see Digital Separations, page 48). The colour blend layers are treated as though they are flat spot colours at this stage, so they are separated from the main image and made pure black by BITMAPPING using 50% threshold.

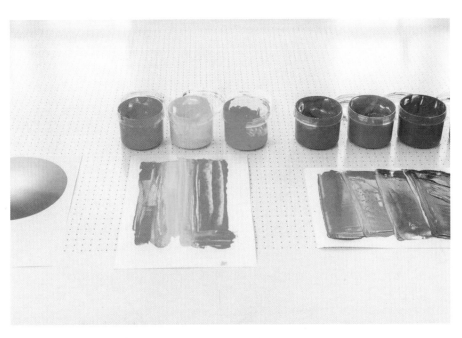

Step 3 – It helps to have a colour wheel to hand when choosing your colours. Ideally, they should merge into each other well and not mix to make a new colour, so opt for colours that sit next to each other on the wheel.

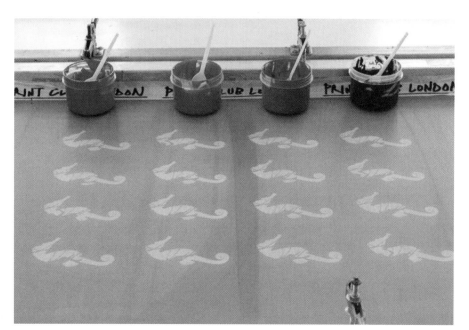

Step 4 – With M.O.L.'s print his second blend layer sits on top of the first in some places. To achieve a good overlay a bit more binder has been used to make the inks more transparent.

Step 5 – The screens are prepared as normal and the materials are gathered. Note is taken of the order of how the layers will be printed so that the screens are put in the right place on the bed. The blend must go horizontally when printing.

Step 6 – To start the blend the ink is positioned at the top of the screen, keeping the colours separate but tapered so that when the squeegee is pulled for the first time, they will blend together.

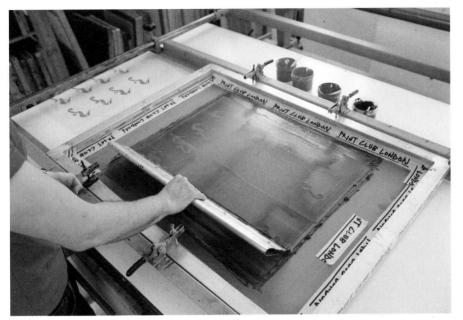

Step 7 – After several pulls, the inks should start to blend together on the screen. The squeegee needs to be straight when pulling and flooding so that it is consistent when printing.

Step 8 – The squeegee can be angled when flooding if the ink needs to move in a certain direction.

Step 9 – Here, M.O.L. is registering his second blend layer onto the print.

After the second blend, a further skin tone and black halftone layer have been added (see the original artwork on page 170). M.O.L. has demonstrated the efficiency of using blends by ending up with such a broad colour palette in his final print.

ORNAMENTAL CONIFER
SIGN-PAINTING POSITIVES

Nicolai Sclater is a Los Angeles-based British sign painter who works under the name Ornamental Conifer. His motto is 'Never perfect but always awesome'. Taking his brush skills to a whole variety of objects, his type has been painted onto walls, leather jackets, windows, helmets, T-shirts, chairs and so much more.

'For this print I decided to use two classic font styles I work with, with a nice electric blue colour for the lower layer. Overlays in fabric-printing can be very tricky but this design allows for some leeway when printing as trapping can be applied to the first layer.'

IF YOU CAN'T

Join them

BEAT THEM

Step 1 – Hand-painted positives are going to be used to make the two-layered T-shirt print. The design is painted onto a sheet of acetate stapled onto a sheet of paper.

Step 2 – Conifer tapes a fresh sheet of acetate on top of the design. This will be the first layer (blue) of the design.

Step 3 – Conifer uses pure black to paint over all of the blue. It is best to paint with a bit of trapping (see the Analogue Artworking section for tips on trapping, page 38) to allow for some wriggle room when the opaque black sits on top.

Step 4 – The next step is to paint the black layer. Conifer has to be careful not to overlap onto the blue lines.

Step 5 – The positives are stuck onto the T-shirt in the same way as when printing a T-shirt (see page 108). They must be layered on top of each other in the way they will sit when printed.

Step 6 – The same process as before is used to ascertain the position of the stencil design correctly on the screens that will be used.

Step 7 – Securely stick down the positives onto the T-shirt on all sides. If both the layers are different sizes, it may be necessary to stick both down separately.

Step 8 – The top black layer is positioned using a ruler. Make sure you use the same size screens when doing this to make measuring and placement easier.

Step 9 – The top layer is taken off the T-shirt and the blue layer is then positioned. Check out the basics of T-shirt printing for more guidance (page 100).

Step 10 – Both screens are exposed using the correct measurements, and then taped up and pin-holed (see page 68). The first layer screen is placed loosely into the arm and will be registered to the T-shirt. As the positives were used to expose with you will need to re-stick them down in the correct position. Or you can use two sets of positives – one set will stay stuck to your T-shirt and the other will be used to expose with.

Step 11 – Align the first layer with the exposed image. If measured correctly, there shouldn't be too much trouble doing this.

Step 12 – Once the screen is aligned, then secure it into the arms with the bolts.

Step 13 – Rather than registering the second screen to a positive stuck down onto your T-shirt, the first layer is going to be printed, and the second layer will be registered to that. This should ensure that every print will be registered perfectly. The first layer's ink has been placed on the screen.

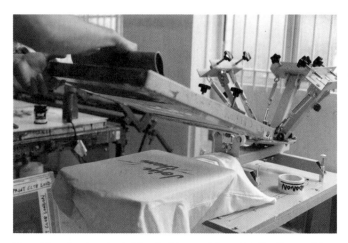

Step 14 – Flood and print the first layer of the print. For tips on this check the section on the basics of T-shirt printing.

Step 15 – Give the screen a couple of heavy floods because the next steps might take a little bit of time. Fabric screens have a lower mesh count so the holes are larger, which means the ink doesn't dry as fast. It is still useful, though, to cover the screen in ink at this stage.

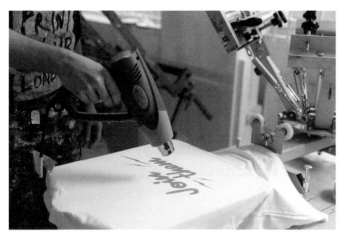

Step 16 – Use a heat gun to make sure that the first layer is dry.

Step 17 – Rotate the arm and loosely position your second screen in place. Carefully register this layer up to the one you've just printed.

Step 18 – Once you are sure it's in place, hold it firmly and tighten the bolts. If everything has been done correctly, the layers will align perfectly when this layer is printed after the first.

Step 19 – Apply ink to the screen and print.

Step 20 – And there you go! A perfectly aligned two-layer print. If you are doing a three- or four-layer print, simply repeat the process of registering to the print, and remember to use the heat gun in between printing.

Step 21 – Don't forget to take your T-shirt off the platen carefully and put it through a conveyor dryer to cure the ink in.

ROB RYAN

PAPERCUTS

Rob Ryan was born in 1962 in Akrotiri in Cyprus and now lives and works in London. He studied fine art at Trent Polytechnic and at the Royal College of Art in London, where he specialized in printmaking. Ryan's intricate paper cut-work can be readily adapted to many other media including ceramics, textiles, homewares and even jewelry. His work often consists of whimsical figures paired with sentimental, grave, honest and occasionally humorous pieces of autobiographical writing.

'I was a screenprinter a long time before I ever began working with cut paper, the medium that my work is best known for. I was always happier drawing and painting on paper than onto canvas or any other surface and I think that this played a part in me becoming a printmaker, it was all about paper. Working on colour separations and cut-out paper stencils gave me an understanding of how screenprinting could work best for me until eventually the paper stencils became the very artwork itself and I concentrated on making my work from cutting silhouettes out of one single sheet. The circle was completed when I began to use my paper cuts as artwork to be directly transferred onto screen without photographic copying or reproduction. This simplicity and purity of intent was one of the aspects of screenprinting that originally appealed to me as an 18-year-old art student.'

13/28   Robert Ryan

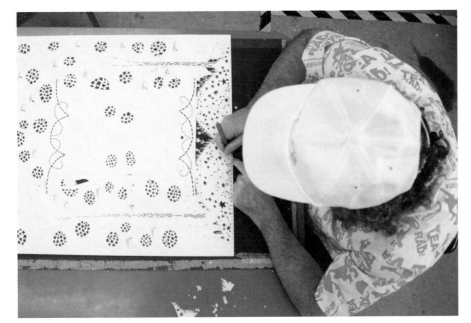

Step 1 – Ryan has drawn the key line image onto a thin sheet of paper and cut out the paper that isn't needed by hand. The paper is thin to allow for ease of cutting, which is a very laborious task.

Step 2 – Because the paper is thin it won't serve well as a positive, so Ryan spray paints the cut-out using a dark paint. This means that when it is exposed onto a screen it will block out the UV light.

Step 3 – The cut-out is exposed onto a screen and then printed in black.

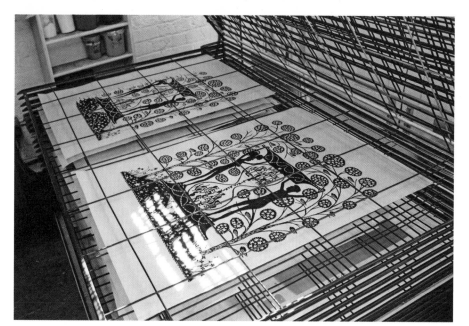

Step 4 – The stencil is printed onto newsprint, which will serve as a base from which the next layers can be cut. A layer is also printed onto transparent paper to be used later for registration purposes.

Step 5 – The first layer will be an overall background colour. Ryan is cutting out the areas to be excluded. This paper is then sprayed as before to make it opaque and it is exposed onto a screen.

Step 6 – This is the first printed layer using the positive that was just made. A colour blend has been used.

Step 7 – The next layer is cut out using one of the newsprint prints made earlier.

Step 8 – Instead of exposing this onto a screen it is stuck onto the underside of it using masking tape. Once the screen has been flooded, the newsprint will stick to the screen and act as a stencil to print through. The printed positive from earlier is then also stuck onto the first colour printed layer, which will help with registration.

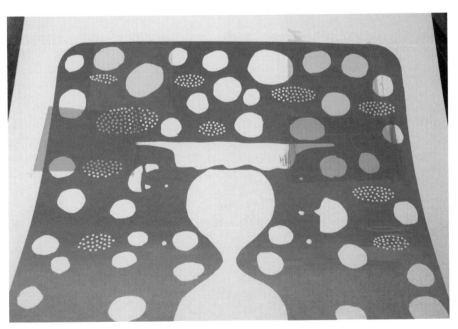

Step 9 – A few colour ways are tested to make sure the colours and transparency of the inks are right.

Rob Ryan: Papercuts   187

Step 10 – Once the inks are right, this colour is then printed onto the edition.

Step 11 – It is important to clean your screen fairly promptly after printing, as keeping the paper stuck to it for too long can damage the mesh.

Step 12 – Going back to the original newsprint prints, the third layer is worked in the same fashion as before.

Step 13 – The next layer is printed in the same way.

Step 14 – The next layer will sit on top of the background layer, so a small test is done beforehand to see what the colour will look like. In this case, the shapes are painted onto the background using gouache.

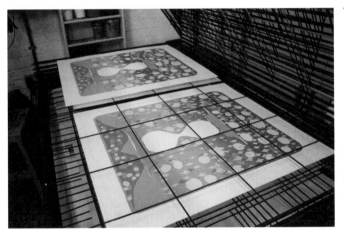

Step 15 – After testing the colour, the next layer is cut and printed in the same way as the previous layers. All of the background layers have been printed.

Step 16 – On the originally exposed screen with the line work on it Ryan has taped off everything but the type and print that has its own layer.

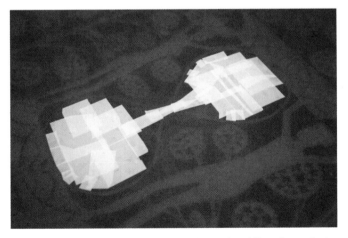

Step 17 – Once printed, the screen is cleaned and then the rest of the line work can be printed. The type is covered up with tape as it has just been printed.

Step 18 – The final line work layer has been printed to bring the whole piece together.

STEVE WILSON
COLOUR OVERLAYS

Steve Wilson is an illustrator who lives and works in Brighton. Originally from North London, Wilson studied illustration at the University of Brighton. He enjoys foraging around local flea markets for obscure books and discarded paraphernalia, which inspire his varied and experimental work. He describes his work as 'somewhere between pop and psychedelic'.

'For this project, I wanted to use an object that had lots of interesting details and could be highlighted and picked out using overlays in printing. This camera was suitable because of the level of detail and fantastic retro aesthetic. Using a combination of overlays and halftones so much detail and a vast range of colour can be achieved. The key is making sure that digitally everything is set up perfectly!'

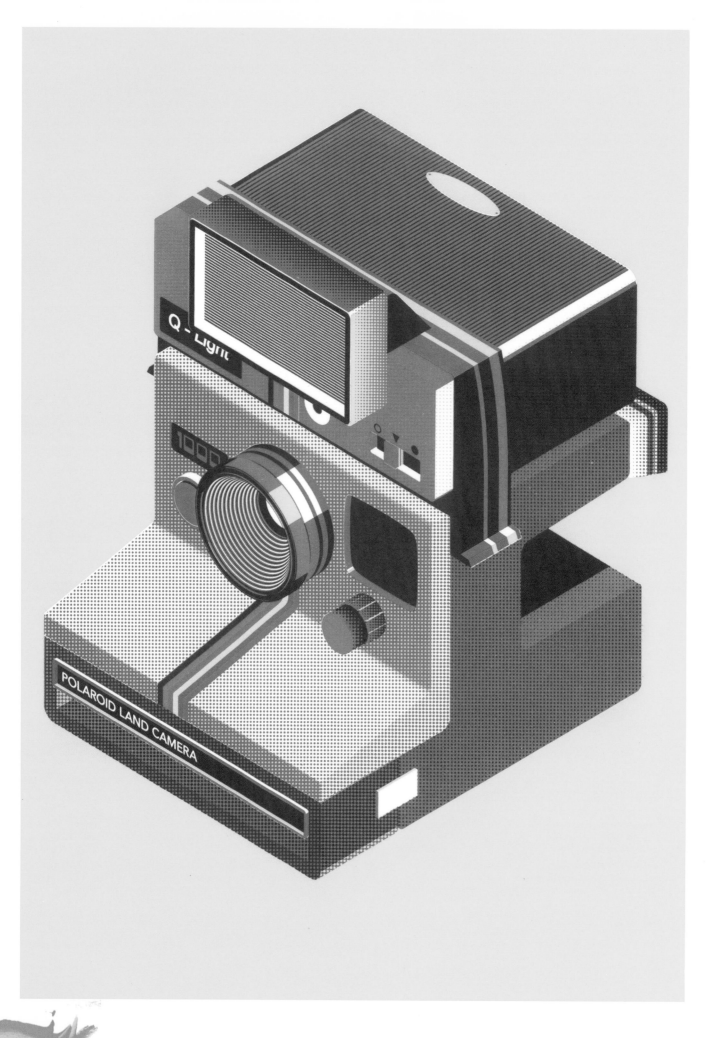

Step 1 – Wilson started by researching imagery and selecting an object for his design. The Polaroid Land Camera was chosen because its dimensions fit well within the 50 x 70 cm (19½ x 27½ in.) paper size that Wilson is working to and it contains some interesting graphic shapes.

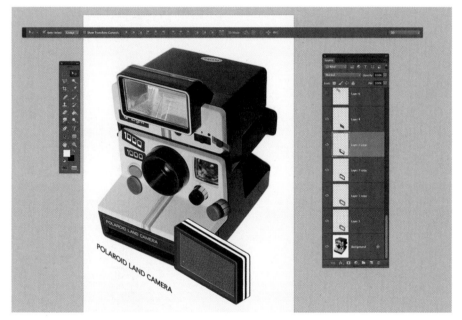

Step 2 – The first stage was to draw an interpretation of the object. Wilson chose to use isometric angles. The individual shapes of the camera were drawn in Adobe Illustrator and then dropped into the Photoshop file one by one, so each piece has its own layer. At this stage four or five of the shapes were dropped into Photoshop over the top of the photograph.

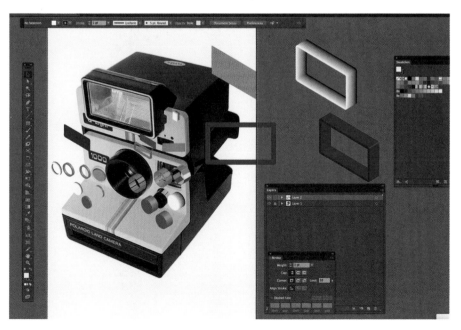

Step 3 – This is a screenshot of the Adobe illustrator file that Wilson is working on alongside the .psd file. All the pieces are drawn individually. In this instance, because the camera is at an isometric angle, he is mostly using the EFFECT > 3D > EXTRUDE and Bevel option from the Illustrator menu bar. A shape is drawn and then extruded using the isometric options within that effect. The shape is then copy and pasted from Illustrator into Photoshop.

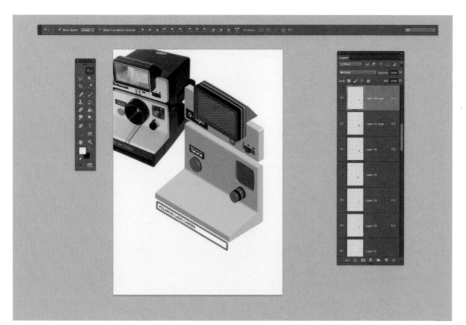

Step 4 – The camera is beginning to take shape in the Photoshop file. At this point the focus is on getting the shapes of the camera right rather than looking at the colours or how to translate it into a screenprint.

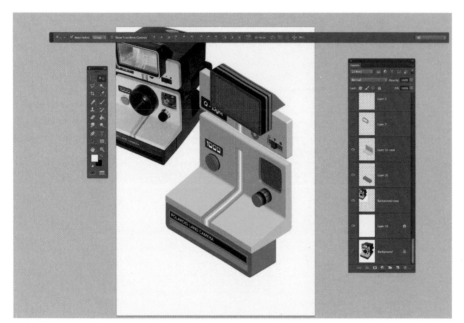

Step 5 – Because the shapes have been created in Adobe Illustrator using the 3D setting they have a lot of gradients and shading. All of those shapes will need to be BITMAPPED later so that it is possible to screenprint them.

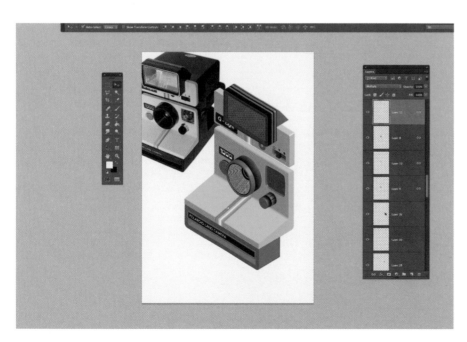

Step 6 – Here, Wilson has started to use patterns, such as the lines within the lens, to help inform the shapes and make the piece feel three-dimensional.

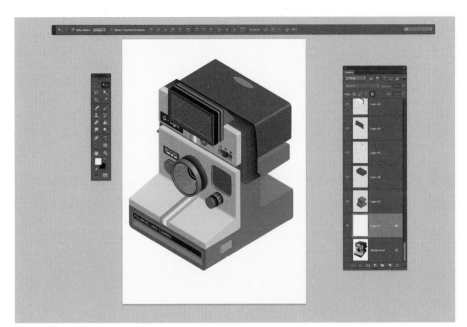

Step 7 – The overall shape of the camera is complete and the isometric drawing of it sits well within the paper format. There are a lot of layers now, as each shape is on its own layer.

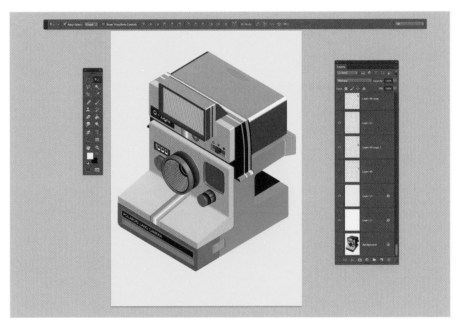

Step 8 – Now that the basic drawing is complete the process of going through each layer of the file and changing the colours begins. Each layer needs to be either pure cyan, magenta or yellow. These colours will give you a red, green, royal blue and also a black when all three (cyan, magenta and yellow) are on top of one another. This is a perfect technique for screenprinting because it means you can screenprint just three layers but your print will look like a seven-colour print.

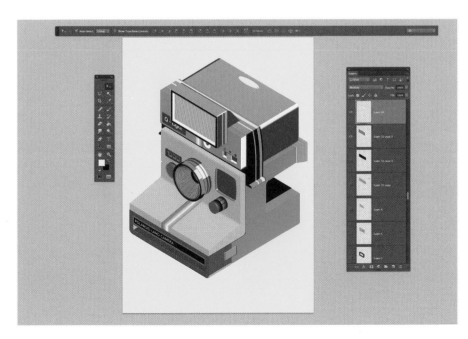

Step 9 – Most of the shapes have now been changed to either cyan, magenta or yellow. The layers are starting to be multiplied on top of one another in the layer settings at the top of the layers box to create a colour reaction with the colours beneath. Some of the shapes made in Illustrator had gradients and shading, which helps inform the dimensionality of the object. It's important not to lose that detail, so certain shapes are converted into halftone dots by BITMAPPING the layer (see page 151). The desired halftone layer must be dragged away from the main file, BITMAPPED and then placed back into it.

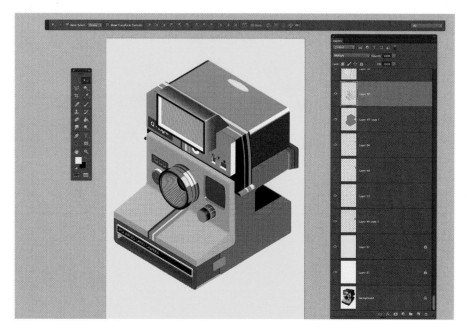

Step 10 – At this point all of the layers are in the correct colours and are multiplied on top of one another. The next step is to merge all of the cyan layers together, then all of the magenta layers and then all of the yellow layers. There will be three layers: a cyan layer, a magenta layer and a yellow layer.

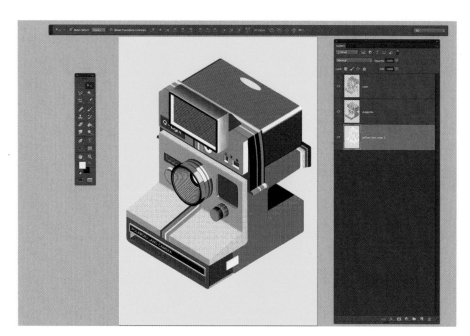

Step 11 – This is the result of combining those layers. The image is now created using just three layers multiplied on top of each other and each layer is a flat colour so that it's ready to screenprint.

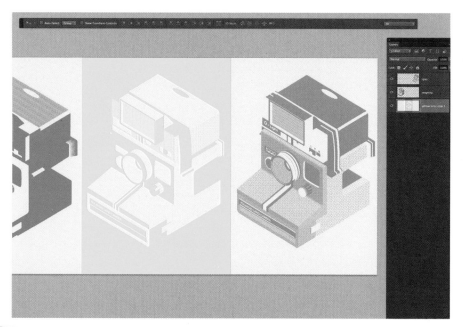

Step 12 – These three layers side by side show the colour separations. They are BITMAPPED so they are pure black and then printed out ready to expose.

Step 13 – Before printing, a colour test was done to make sure the colours would overlay properly. A small test screen has been made up and each colour is printed onto a small bit of paper.

Step 14 – By printing each layer on top of each other you can clearly see how the final colours will look. The printing can proceed once this looks right. Otherwise adjustments may need to be made. It might be that your ink needs to be made more transparent by using binder or a screenprinting medium.

Step 15 – Now it's time to start printing the final piece. The yellow normally goes down first because it's the lightest.

Step 16 – Yellow is quite bright so make sure everything is coming through properly when printing.

Step 17 – Here is the yellow layer printed.

Step 18 – Next is the magenta layer.

Step 19 – Even if the inks have been tested beforehand, it's important to make sure the overlay is really working its magic at this point.

Step 20 – Once the magenta layer looks good, then it's time for the last layer, the cyan.

Step 21 – Here is the finished print.

SUSIE WRIGHT
HAND-DRAWN POSITIVES

Susie Wright is an illustrator and printmaker from Edinburgh. She studied illustration at Edinburgh College of Art and graduated with an MA in communication design from Central Saint Martins, London, in 2006. Her work explores the landscape, architecture, wildlife and flora around her.

'Making hand-made positives and printing is a good organic process. It starts with an original drawing but can easily change as the various layers are built up on top of each other. Materials you will need: heavyweight drawing film, heavyweight trace, black acrylic paint, a selection of brushes, fine liners, pencils, an etching tool or needle, masking tape, and a light box.'

Step 1 – Wright is drawing three detailed budgies, which will be turned into a five-layer print. The drawing will be used as a key for making the hand-made positives so it must be the same size as the intended final print.

Step 2 – To make the positives, Wright puts a sheet of the heavyweight drawing film over the original drawing and fixes it down with masking tape.

Step 3 – The first layer is painted with a brush and black acrylic paint. The first layer is blue, which will be combined with another layer of yellow to make the green of the budgies. It is important that a fairly thick layer of the acrylic is used to block the light out when exposing.

Step 4 – The yellow layer is painted. To give it a bit of texture, Wright scratches away paint from the acrylic on the positive using an etching tool. It is easier to work in reverse this way as thin detailed lines can be achieved easily and quickly rather than trying to paint acrylic and leave thin gaps.

Step 5 – The blue and yellow layers are printed; these will be used to keep working over along with the original drawing. Sometimes it can be hard to work on many black positives when they are layered up together.

Step 6 – Another grey layer and a beige layer have been drawn up using the same technique as before of creating ink drawings with small details scratched out. They are exposed and printed.

Step 7 – The black layer is hand-drawn rather than painted on, so Wright has used tracing paper rather than heavyweight drawing film to get a thinner line. The original drawing is used as the reference point for the drawing.

TIPS

Tracing paper will wrinkle if you are using water-based inks, but if you are using heavyweight drawing film it won't. If you want to show a bit of texture on the positives, try using a textured drafting film.

Step 8 – The drawing is placed on top of the print in case any additions need to be made.

Step 9 – The black layer is printed.

Susie Wright: Hand-drawn Positives   205

THOMAS WHITCOMBE

PHOTO TO CMYK

Thomas Whitcombe is a graphic designer and printmaker based in London. Originally from Glastonbury in Somerset, Whitcombe is inspired by the natural world – its landscapes, flora, fauna and creatures. An avid collector of second-hand reference books and photography, his work explores the juxtaposition between the natural and built environments. Pieces are shaped by evocative images, explored using illustration, collage and photography, and ultimately a little bit of joy.

'As a process, CMYK screenprinting appeals to my love of vibrant colours, allowing a full and unlimited range which does justice to my found images and is a great way to reproduce physical collages. A CYMK print is a print made up of four layers of ink: cyan, magenta, yellow and key (black). By halftoning your image correctly using these four colours you can print photographic images that appear to have the full spectrum of colour contained within!'

Step 1 – Whitcombe made this digital photographic collage.

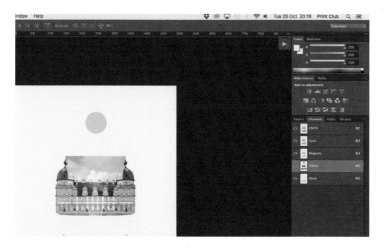

Step 2 – Click on IMAGE > MODE to make sure you're working in the CMYK colour profile. This is the time to tweak the colours if necessary.

Step 3 – Click on the CHANNELS button next to the LAYERS button. There are five layers: cyan, magenta, yellow and black, with a CMYK layer at the top.

Step 4 – Each of the four layers needs to be HALFTONED separately. By clicking on the eye icon you can remove the chosen layers to leave just one, in this case the cyan layer. At this point you can either open up a new document and copy this layer or BITMAP, save your image and then start again from your original .psd file. Each of the four layers must be HALFTONED using a different angle from each other to get the best effect. They must, however, all use the same shape and frequency (see page 166 for more information on using frequencies). Whitcombe has used a frequency of 33 throughout and kept the shape as round. The cyan layer should be BITMAPPED at an angle of 15 degrees.

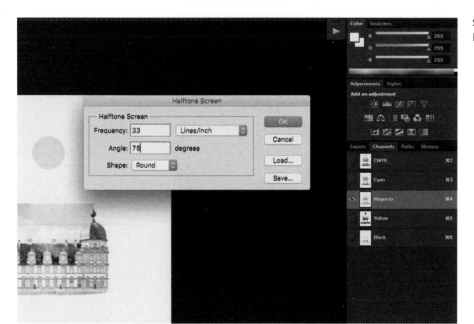

Step 5 – The magenta layer should be BITMAPPED with an angle of 75 degrees.

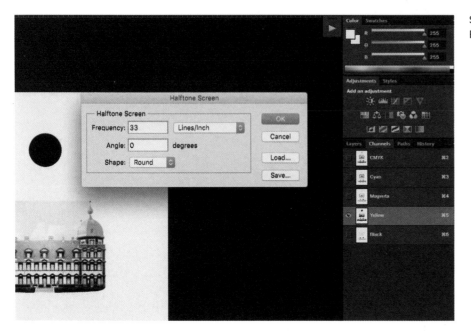

Step 6 – The yellow layer must be BITMAPPED with an angle of 0 degrees.

Step 7 – The black must be BITMAPPED with an angle of 45 degrees. By bitmapping all of the layers with different angles the colours will sit side by side when printing rather than on top of each other. If the angles are all the same, often one colour can come out looking too dominant, or the colours overlay each other too much and the image can appear much darker than it should. The layers are ready to be made into positives and printed.

Step 8 – Registration marks have been used on this print to line up the first two layers. The layer that goes down is the yellow. Sometimes this can be very faint and hard for the next layer – the cyan – to register to.

Step 9 – The yellow goes down.

TIPS

Sometimes the positives are exposed onto the screens at a slight angle. This can often reduce the effect of a potential moire pattern on the eyes.

Step 10 – Next is the cyan.

Step 11 – Here is the print with the yellow and cyan layers on it. Normally at this point the print will be made mostly of yellow, blues and greens.

Step 12 – The magenta goes down next.

Step 13 – A lot more depth should be visible in the image after the magenta goes down; any reds and oranges will have appeared.

Step 14 – It's time for the last layer: the black.

Step 15 – The black layer should have put the final punch and depth into the image.

PRINTING OUTSIDE THE BOX

BOB GILL

HAND FINISHED WITH WATERCOLOUR

Bob Gill is an American designer, illustrator, writer, filmmaker and teacher. He was the Gill in Fletcher/Forbes/Gill, which eventually became Pentagram. He was elected into the New York Art Directors' Club Hall of Fame and was presented with a Lifetime Achievement Award by the D&AD.

Here Bob Gill has hand finished his prints with watercolour painting after printing. This detailing makes each print unique despite being part of an edition.

CASPAR WILLIAMSON

GLOW IN THE DARK

Caspar Williamson is heavily involved in the printmaking scene in the UK. He lectures on the subject and has taught both corporate and educational workshops throughout the UK. He has also exhibited widely and is represented by several galleries.

Here Williamson has used glow-in-the-dark ink (phosphorescent). It is fairly easy to get hold of, however, the quality (in terms of the brightness) does vary from product to product. The ink is made up of phosphor particles and a clear base solution. A phosphor is a substance that radiates visible light after being energized. Phosphors come in all colours, but because the human eye can see green far more easily than other colours, most glow-in-the-dark products come in green. Depending on the manufacturer, different quantities of the phosphors are used and different types, which vary in brightness. Inks ordered directly from manufacturers tend to work better as higher ratios of phosphors can be requested. The glow effect works more effectively when printed onto a lighter colour – white has the greatest impact when the lights are off! It is advisable to use a wide-meshed screen when printing, as you want to avoid sieving out any phosphor particles.

JOE CRUZ

HAND FINISHED WITH PASTEL

Joe Cruz is a visual artist whose work spans art, design, fashion and graphics. He was born in London in 1988 and has a multi-cultural background, with family from France, Spain, Austria and England. He graduated from the Norwich School of Art and Design in 2010. Cruz uses expressive lines, strong colours and graphic imagery within his work. He is fascinated by bold, simple statements, as seen in political posters and advertising slogans. Simple and subversive messages play a key role in his work. He loves working with found imagery, juxtaposing it with bold, colourful and strong marks to give the work a contemporary context.

This piece is a single-layer black screenprint finished off with hand-made chalk marks. It is part of an edition, but because the artist's personal hand-made marks are included, each piece is unique in its own way.

THE SOFT CITY
PRINTING ON BOOKS

The Soft City is East London artist Daniel Speight's pseudonym. Speight's current 'Book Block' project is street art in the most literal sense – illustrations of the city's streets are screenprinted directly onto the sides of reclaimed books. Combining the digital and the hand-made, 'Book Block' transforms shelves into streets, breathing new life into old reading material. The results are considered pieces of work that draw a new connection between the materials and space around us. Books and cities both hold stories.

Here, Speight has printed an intricate design onto the side of books using a complex clamping system. Very tightly registered layers of ink are printed onto books that have been trimmed down so they are smooth and level with each other.

GUY GATIER
PRINTING ON GLASS

Guy Gatier graduated from Reading University. He has developed a well-balanced and thorough understanding of the printing process, with an ability to work with all media such as paper, wood and fabric.

This print is extremely intricate. It has 18 layers printed on glass with a mirror background. It was made to celebrate the prediction in the film *Back to the Future* of what 2015 would be like. The print has one design on the front and another on the back, which can only be seen from an angle in the mirror background. It requires a lot of work to get all of the layers in the right order.

LOVENSKATE

SKATEBOARD PRINTING

Lovenskate is an East London-based screenprinter who specializes in a unique method of printing directly onto skateboards. It involves using specially shaped screens and squeegees to contour to the shape of the board and print all the way down it.

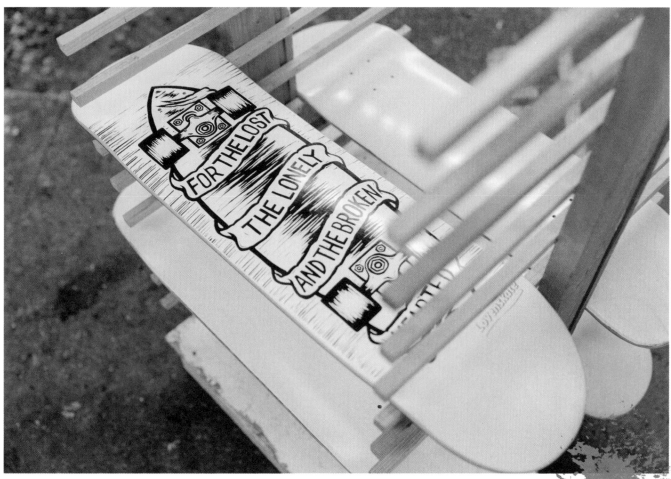

PURE EVIL

FINISHING TOUCHES

Charles Uzzell-Edwards is a graffiti and street artist better
known by the cheeky moniker Pure Evil. His tag is a vampire
bunny rabbit that was born out of his feeling of remorse after
shooting a rabbit in the countryside as a youth. He explains that
he's always regretted this terrible deed and feels that the rabbit
is coming back to haunt him.

In this piece of work, Pure Evil has screenprinted a background
and then drawn straight onto the glass after it has been
framed. The eye drip has been printed onto the paper, but he
has extended the drip onto the frame and even onto the wall
behind it.

DONK

PASTE UP

Donk is a street artist who works within the paste-up tradition. He combines original photography, printmaking and hand-finishing techniques. He has been placing his work onto the streets of London and elsewhere since 2008. His images are often inhabited by his family and friends, who take on the various roles within his work. The strongly evocative and anachronistic images remix urban history and culture, across a timeline of his own making, which reference the past and the contemporary to make playful connections between universal themes of human strength, vulnerability and the passage of time.

The paste-up here was made by screenprinting onto thin paper and then applying it to a wall using wheat paste.

MAKING IT

ANTHONY PETERS

SCREENPRINTING IN THE 21ST CENTURY

Anthony Peters is a designer, printmaker and filmmaker from the south coast of England. He designs under the aliases Imeus and Wow & Flutter. He also makes up one third of the film production company Look and Yes.

In 2015 he co-directed *Made You Look*, a feature documentary about the UK graphic arts scene that starred many of the key figures in the UK scene, including Anthony Burrill, Hattie Stewart, Peepshow Collective and Print Club.

BECOME A MICROSCOPE
— Sister Corita Kent

Each creative generation is given certain parameters to work within at birth. The surrounding culture, geography, politics, people and developments in technology all form the basis on which the artist views the world; both aesthetically and in terms of content.

To one iconic US West Coast nun in the early 1960s, these conditions were incredibly fertile. Across the nation a new and unique aesthetic was emerging: Pop Art. Sister Corita Kent was something of an anomaly within the art world of the early 1960s. She was a Roman Catholic nun in the order of Sisters of the Immaculate Heart of Mary, a celebrated humanist, art teacher and serigrapher (that's a screenprinter to you and me). Sister Corita's work truly acted as a mirror to the turbulent times in which she lived. In a true pop art style she used the medium of screenprinting to create big, bold artworks espousing messages of hope and love. No area of culture was off-limits and subjects covered included the Vietnam War, civil rights struggles and the countless assassinations of the era. Nothing escaped her gaze, and in her aesthetic she would use fragments of American visual culture: road signs, packaging, newspapers, magazines, car washes. She would break these into pure block-colours to be printed en masse almost in the same way protest posters would be 'manufactured' and posted across cities.

Sister Corita's ideas and aesthetics were very much in the mould of her contemporaries Charles and Ray Eames and Buckminster Fuller, all of whom shared a love of accessible ideas that benefitted the wider populace. Screenprinting was not a nostalgic craft form in the time of Sister Corita, it was a contemporary technology and one of the best ways for artists to make multiples and to experiment with colours and shapes with ease. As is always the case, the new technology was an integral part of a new creative development.

YOU KNOW THAT THE PRESIDENT DRINKS COKE, LIZ TAYLOR DRINKS COKE, AND JUST THINK, YOU CAN DRINK COKE, TOO. A COKE IS A COKE AND NO AMOUNT OF MONEY CAN GET YOU A BETTER COKE THAN THE ONE THE BUM ON THE CORNER IS DRINKING.
— Andy Warhol

At the same time on the opposite coast Andy Warhol was ten or so years into his career as an artist, but was just beginning to exhibit works using screenprinting as the core medium.

Warhol was also mirroring the times, as Sister Corita had, with his take on mass production and Fordism. He was enamoured with the idea that capitalism made everyone equal – that this was a kind of communist utopia borne out of mass market consumerism.

Screenprinting was the perfect medium to replicate the production line of industrial scale manufacturing. Warhol even went as far as to call his studio the Factory.

Warhol and the Pop Art movement created the art 'industry' as we know it. Multiples meant more sales for less work. Modern technology offered speed and efficiency, yet still preserved individuality with the hand of the artist upon each screenprint, since all artworks were hand-finished with painted areas. Creativity had become commodity.

LA BEAUTÉ EST DANS LA RUE
— Paris '68 slogan

In a different continent later that decade, screenprinting was used as a medium for social change. Paris 1968: students, factory workers, newspaper publishers, print shops, office workers, fishermen and transport workers were among the 11 million who went on strike in protest over wages, working conditions and student rights. During the strikes and disruptions, a handful of art students who went by the name of Atelier Populaire used silk-screenprinting to help spread the messages of the people throughout the streets and factories of Paris and beyond. Striking newspaper and print shop workers contributed paper and ink, and no one would claim responsibility for authorship over the poster designs. The purpose was not to promote the individual ego but to fight a greater cause. One colour was the preference, usually red or black. The high-gloss, mass-manufactured varnish Warhol aspired to was long gone. Instead the printing was rough and ready, favoured for its bold aesthetic and ease of replication; sometimes up to 2,000 posters could be made in an evening. This was pure communication: art and commerce were not a consideration. Screenprinted posters were cheap to replicate and paste up across a city divided. People needed to know what was happening, and the streets sang with the voices of protest – glorious, bold, and not for sale!

THIS IS A CHORD, THIS IS ANOTHER, THIS IS A THIRD. NOW FORM A BAND
— Sideburns Fanzine, 1977

Times changed and protest changed too. On the streets of England in the late 1970s, people were tired of power cuts and poverty, refuse collectors were on strike, riots and strikes broke out up and down the country and people were generally sick and tired of the way they were governed. A new youth culture emerged. Punk and Post Punk were a rejection of everything that came before. The aesthetics were rough and ready: clothes were hand-made and the music was three-chord rock 'n' roll on cheap instruments. Print beds, screens and squeegees were abandoned

28/100

AP II/III   [signature]

as new technology meant that paper sleeves for 7"s, fanzines and posters could easily be replicated on photocopiers. Screenprinting was out of favour.

Forty years later, by rights this book shouldn't exist. Giclée digital print technology can effectively print high-quality artworks with much less physical effort than silk-screenprinting. Plus social media has stepped in where once activists and punks made posters or fanzines in order to communicate a message or to rally the troops. Every purpose that screenprinting fulfilled has been replaced... So why is screenprinting still here?

Changes in technology in the 21st century have had an unanticipated effect. Whereas previous technological developments have been a catalyst for artistic evolution, the internet era has created a kind of creative allergic reaction. Our lives are lived at high speed. We don't have a tactile relationship to the digital world, we move from screen to screen, not touching or owning anything, and everything is perfect unless it is programmed otherwise. We even have computers making art: check out the hallucinatory worlds created by Google Deep Dream and algorithmic art such as the incredible projects created by Eric Drass/Shardcore, where computers are given a set of parameters that allow for a limited kind of creativity. The results are astounding.

The problem is that technology has become too fast, too inhuman. A dormant need to be among tactile, real objects seems to have awoken in many people. We all long to slow down. This has brought about entire movements based on getting away from the 24/7 information feed we get from our computers. I love the slow culture movement, in particular Norway's Slow TV, the antidote to fast editing and rolling plots. It aims to inspire us to step outside and actually take a look at what's around us, and to reconnect with something physical, something tactile, such as the bark of a tree or a beautiful 300gsm uncoated paper.

Consider the physical actions you undertake when making things on a computer. Be it with a mouse or a Wacom tablet, you use the same actions for everything you do, whether updating spreadsheets, designing posters, writing emails, surfing the web, checking your bank balance, writing a novel or designing a typeface. It's all the same movement – the swipe of a mouse, the click of a button, the tap of the keyboard. We lose important synaptic relationships when the mental task changes but the physical task remains the same. Screenprinting, painting, drawing, typesetting, lino-cutting; all these things have their own, very different physicality, and I think this is incredibly good for our mental well-being.

Not only are more people now making things by hand, but buying hand-made goods has never been more popular either. The internet has been an extraordinary bedfellow for modern creativity. So many printers, illustrators, artists and designers now have the ability to connect with an audience without having to go through a curator or taste-maker. As such, the maker is selling directly to an audience, and creatives no longer have to be in a big city to have a career. Over 20 million hand-made items are sold on Etsy alone every year, with around 4.5 billion page views to boot, and countless other similar sites exist. People may be going offline to create things, but a whole generation of makers are now entrepreneurs, shop owners and even employers, and while we may be seeing a dwindling independent high street in a physical sense, it seems that independent business online has never been so strong.

So the screenprinting movement of the last 10 years is part of, and indeed spearheading, a return to getting inky, celebrating imperfection, working hard for your creativity and mastering a skill that doesn't have an undo button. The vectors and bezier curves have been set aside and replaced with the smell of ink and the pull of a squeegee as the ink bleeds onto paper. Mistakes are celebrated and often a mistake becomes a style – we learn from getting it wrong and from practising over and over. Most importantly, we forget about our emails, our social media accounts, the barrage of bad news that we are bombarded with every day, and we exist in the moment, a beautiful inky moment. We reclaim some much needed time for ourselves.

DAVE BUONAGUIDI
MAKING MONEY

Born in London in 1964, Dave Buonaguidi has spent over 30 years in advertising. He created the iconic *Make Tea not War* poster for the anti-Iraq War march in 2003. It is now part of the collection at the Victoria & Albert Museum in London and hangs in the Museum of Modern and Contemporary Art of Trento and Rovereto in Italy. He began screenprinting in 2015 and has been horribly addicted ever since.

I have spent over 30 years working in creative industries, but I was over 50 when I rediscovered screenprinting.

As a creative thinker, I was always coming up with tons of ideas, but the problem I had was that I had no outlet because I didn't know how to produce anything. When I learned how to screenprint I found it was something that would unlock a lot of my creative blockages. Learning how to print enabled me to complete and reproduce a huge number of the ideas that would otherwise still be festering in my metaphorical mental plan chest.

In advertising you have to think very conceptually and very commercially.

That's our job.

We are paid by our clients to improve their business and make them money.

And as a result of this commercial relationship we have very strong processes to guide us.

The process is essential to keeping us on track and focused:

1. We begin with a brief: we work out what we are going to say, who we are saying it to, and why.
2. We analyse and understand the audience: what do they like?, where do they live?, and what do they do?

3. We then try to create something that will cut through all the other shit that's out there and engage with this audience.

We use the semi-scientific approach because there are huge sums of money at stake and because it costs so much money to create and then put advertising work out there – we have to be semi-sure it will work.

It is essential that we create something that will connect to that audience. As an example, creating an idea that is funny or emotional can be a very powerful way to help connect people to your brand.

When I began printing, I was very clear that I was not doing this for fun. I am an adfuck and obviously very commercial, so I wanted to be successful, and that meant selling lots of work.

Strangely, being commercial is something that some artists struggle with. I know some who feel as though they are sell-outs if they sell too much and if they sell none at all they feel like failures. So they live in the middle, being neither one nor the other.

I want to stress, DO NOT be ashamed of making money out of a talent that you have. Enjoy it and relish it because there is no better feeling than making a living out of doing something that you love.

When I first began screenprinting, I talked to Kate, who runs the gallery at Print Club, and I asked her, 'Tell me what sells.' I remember that she was quite surprised that I asked because I think what tends to happen is that artists often have very little in the way of guidance or mentoring: they have a style and they make what they want to, and they don't connect the dots between what they want to do and what people will buy.

Doing what you want to do is all well and good, but it leads to two scenarios:

The artist is creating stuff that people like. Woohoo! It's happy days for the gallery and the artist.

The artist is creating stuff that is not popular. Oh shit! That is no good for anyone, and any gallery will drop you like a squirrel-shit sandwich. Kate's response to my question actually surprised me.

'Pineapples and parrots,' she said.

But then again, it's not that big a surprise to see that the two most popular sellers had 'a sort of' emotional connection to most people.

People like pineapples – they are interesting-looking, exotic, they apparently bring fortune, and pretty much everyone has at some stage eaten one and felt good afterwards. People also like parrots – they are colourful, exotic, beautiful, and pretty much everyone has felt good after seeing one.

Pineapples and parrots. They're a bit boring, but what's not to like?

Now, if you are just printing for a laugh because you are independently wealthy and don't really need the extra cash, you can probably stop reading this now.

But if you want to make stuff, hopefully sell it and then make money, enjoy your life, buy things that you like and have fun being someone in control of their own destiny then read on.*

*I would just like to stress that I am by no stretch of the imagination a successful artist, but there are lots of things I have learned over the last couple of years of selling that, combined with my experience as a commercial adfuck, might be useful.

BUILD A RELATIONSHIP WITH YOUR GALLERY

Sure, they often take 50% of whatever you make, but your job is to make sure you get them working as hard as they can for YOU.

If you make something that will sell a lot, they will work really hard to sell it for you because the more money you make, the more money they make. Become business partners. Ask them for advice, constantly talk to them about things you are doing and trying. Talk to them about opportunities. Make them think you are an energy source and good at what you do and they will bend over backwards to make money out of you.

ALWAYS BE INDUSTRIOUS

Make sure you are always doing new things. To create is to make. Not everything you make will be a massive seller, but your purpose is to create.

If you make something that doesn't sell, stop moaning, get over it quickly, and move on. If you make something that is a massive seller, don't get complacent, move on and create another big seller.

Again, this is a good signal to send to your gallery, fresh and new is a very compelling story for a gallery to talk about, and it keeps you inventing and improving and developing your style.

TRY TO CREATE A BRAND

You and your personality are as important as the work you create, so make sure there is some of you in all the work you make. What's the story behind what you do? Sometimes the story and how you tell that story can be just as interesting as the work itself.

ALWAYS TRY TO INNOVATE

Look at any great artists, and you will see their work transition and develop over their careers. It's important that you do the same: it keeps you fresh and scared, doing stuff you have never done before is very stimulating and exciting and will make you better at managing and developing your personal style. It's also another thing that galleries really like.

DON'T JUST PRINT SOMETHING BECAUSE YOU LIKE IT

Print for the people who will potentially buy it.

Obviously, you have to make sure it's something you like, but always try to put yourself in the mindset of someone who might be interested in buying your work. Think about the way the advertising process works and try to apply it to your own work:

Who do you want to sell to, and why?
What do they like?
What will cut through the clutter and stand out?

MAKE IT NOISY

PR and social media are very powerful tools and relatively easy to build and make the most of. Most of us are social, we have social media presences, but social media does demand constant attention, and you must work at it. Talking about stuff you are working on, stuff you are printing, stuff you have printed, stuff you have seen, old stuff, and new stuff, everything you send out and talk about helps to build your brand, and if you have a brand you will sell more.

MAKE IT EVEN NOISIER

Doing something cheeky, borderline illegal, totally illegal or even downright disgusting is not always a bad thing. Think of the most memorable culture you have seen and why it was memorable: often there is controversy somewhere in there. It helps cut through all the other shit out there. As an example, Damien Hirst and Banksy have played the controversy card very well to build their brands. Pineapples and parrots might sell well, but they are a bit vanilla. Would the artist's brand do better with a little more edge?

I think so. I like edge.

INVENT DESIRE

Art is like Marmite, you either love it or hate it, and I have overestimated my own desirability dozens of times. I have created a nice design (or so I thought), printed an edition of 50, thinking about all the money I'm going to make, and ended up selling two. In fact, I have so many unsold prints lying about that it's embarrassing.

Ultimately, the amount you create depends on the way you work. If you print two editions a year, and you sell slowly but surely, then go ahead and print big editions.

If you're like me and create lots and lots of stuff, then print more shit, but in shorter editions. I actually think a 'when it's gone it's gone' mentality is more exciting and compelling. Create a brand, and then add the short-fast-edition mentality and people will often want to buy your stuff because you did it, as much as buying your stuff because they like it.

BE CONFIDENT

If you are creative and know how to make shit, get a T-shirt printed because believe me that is a real skill to be proud of, especially in the world we live in now that is over populated with lazy no-marks who just want to be famous for being famous. Kim Kardashian is all very good and that, but she doesn't do much apart from get her big bum out all the time.

You are valuable because you make stuff, you are creative. You want and need to make stuff. So go out and make lots of stuff. Then add to your confidence by selling your stuff to other people. It's a wonderful boost and will inspire you to keep going and do it more and more.

A word of warning: just don't turn into an asshole and get arrogant.

No one likes an asshole.

MAKE SURE YOU HAVE FUN.

In an ideal world, making cool shit would be your day job, right? But most of us have other jobs and make cool shit on weekends and evenings because it's what we love. Doing something you love is an amazing thing, doing something you love that makes you money is even better. Have as much fun as possible. Of course, you will do some things that you prefer to others, but you are creative, you are always moving forward and innovating, and that is the most fun you can have.

Enjoy.

LUCILLE CLERC
YOUR PRESENCE ON SOCIAL MEDIA

Lucille Clerc is a French graphic designer and illustrator based in London. She set up her studio after graduating from Central Saint Martins, London, with an MA in communication design. She works predominantly as a designer and illustrator for books and magazines, but also for the fashion industry, and occasionally designs interior or exhibition spaces. Some of her clients include the Victoria & Albert Museum, London, Fortnum & Mason, Farrow & Ball, Berluti, Magma bookstore and Marks & Spencer, as well as various magazines. Her work has been regularly exhibited across Europe.

In terms of social media, I mainly use Instagram. My approach to using the app is as though it is a dialogue between friends: I use it to raise questions such as 'did you see this?', 'what do you think of that?', etc. I share my personal work, motivational images or thoughts about news and the way we live in Europe. I also post sketches from trips and visits to museums and places I love in France or in the UK. Occasionally, I also share illustrations I do for press when I feel this could raise attention about issues that are important to me (social equality, environment, architectural mutations). It's a visual diary.

Apart from when I do shows, as an artist, I rarely get the opportunity to speak to people who have an interest in my work, especially if they live on the other side of the planet. I really value exchanging ideas directly with people I wouldn't have met otherwise. In my practice it is very important that I keep drawing for myself, just because I enjoy it, free from any commercial purpose. It is something I've always liked doing since being a child and it's important to reconnect with that side of things, experimenting, making mistakes, so my Instagram sometimes becomes like a mini lab, which I love! It helps me discover new ideas, and shows very quickly a variety of things you can do without the constraints of a website. It's a healthy balance, similar to warming up when you play an instrument.

Most of my work is produced physically as screenprints at Print Club. Screenprinting is such a beautiful craft and yet the process itself is rather unseen to the general public. Unless you witness the different steps it can be difficult to imagine all the work needed to produce a single multi-layered print. This is what makes each print so special and is the reason why we spend so many hours in the studio trying to refine our skills. Ultimately this is what adds value to the work. I started showing the process behind mine, from sketching to printing. Since I work mainly in CMYK recording and watching the overlapping of layers and colours mixing makes it easier to explain and share my passion for this craft. It's also nice to share how the studio works, the machines and tools, but also the people who make it a nice place to work and share ideas.

I didn't start using Instagram with the intent of 'getting noticed', although I am grateful that it has now benefitted me in that way. Some of the discussions I had with people thanks to it have changed the way I see social media in a very positive way. This gave me the confidence to stay true to my style and ideas. So I stick to that in a genuine way and I think this is why people find and follow my feed. It interests me to keep producing images crafted as if they were commissions, but on themes that wouldn't necessarily find a space on the market. It's a very special feeling to realize that an image you've produced touches people and finds an echo. An image will always have more power than words and as image makers we have a responsibility in what we show, what we tolerate, support, or refuse. We can use this power to shake things up, even if only a tiny bit within our circle.

JO HAM

BRANDING YOURSELF

Jo Ham is the illustrator and founder of the homeware brand HAM. After graduating from the Ruskin School of Art, Oxford University, where she gained a degree in fine art with a specialism in anatomy, she started working in branding at the design consultancy Wolff Olins. In 2011 she formed her eponymous studio and has since exhibited with Liberty, Designjunction, Mother, Billy Name and Colette Paris and created bespoke artwork for Nike, Eurostar, West Elm and Maggie's Centres.

Ham's work seeks to celebrate the everyday. Informed by her studies and early career as a brand strategist, she has always been fascinated by popular culture and the zeitgeist, in particular life's simple pleasures and how we interact with one another through work and play.

HAM follows the contented life of Rabbit, capturing his daily adventures, sporting escapades and social outings in silhouette form on a range of thoughtfully crafted ceramics, wall art and paper goods.

HAM's debut homeware collection of ceramics and fabrics was first picked up by Liberty in London and has since been exhibited in London, New York and Paris. Featured on the pages of international magazines, it can now be found on the shelves of leading retailers around the world.

Making It

WHAT IS BRAND?

Brand is not just the way your company looks. Of course, having brilliant business cards, a website and a logo is absolutely vital in how you portray yourself, but if you can also truly nail the broader concept of branding, it can really make the difference between good and great.

Marketers talk about 'identifying your brand idea', 'finding your guiding principle' and making a list of 'brand values'. All this really means is knowing what you're about and what makes you different.

Before I started HAM, I worked in branding, helping companies figure out what they stood for and how they could use that understanding to grow. We had strategies, research, budgets and time to plan and implement ideas. And we saw results – there was no doubt it worked. So, when I left to start my own business I knew how important it was to embrace branding early and I got stuck into planning. Weeks of procrastination followed and it quickly became apparent that turning all the theories into practice was tough. There was so much else to do, cash was scarce and my business idea consisted of a piece of paper and a rabbit sketch! This was going to be harder than I thought.

In this chapter I'm going to share a little bit about my journey, how I got to grips with brand and some of the things I've learnt along the way about branding a small business.

THE CORE IDEA

If I put you on the spot right now and asked you to tell me in one sentence what your business was about, could you? I struggled with this when I started out, stumbling around being British-made and something to do with drawing animals. It soon became clear that if I didn't know what I stood for, my customers definitely weren't going to understand what I was trying to sell them.

So, how do you start to clarify and articulate your own idea? It will of course evolve over time – the more you make and live with your brand, the more you will fine-tune it and really get under the skin of what you are about. So don't put yourself under too much pressure to have it all done and dusted in a week.

Grab a piece of paper and write down all the things that describe what you do and why it's special – everything and anything that pops into your head. Are you about humour, craftsmanship, Britishness, fun, texture, upbeat vibes, luxury, neon, weirdness, minimal design, seriousness, cuteness...? You get my drift. Start to prioritize that list and pull out the words that really resonate. And then go to your friends and family, and to their friends and family, and ask them the same questions and see what you get back. Start to build a picture in words about your creativity, fine-tuning the headlines whenever you get feedback or have time to reflect.

BE DIFFERENT

When you've begun to button down what you're about and how you are different, get onto Google and make sure that you are being original and not treading on anyone's toes. Look at your potential competitors. If you find someone out there already saying or making something similar to what you want to do, think long and hard about whether to proceed with that idea. Copying is a definite no-no, but sometimes you may unknowingly create something similar. Don't hide from this. Whatever the circumstance, there is no real benefit to pushing ahead with an idea or a concept that isn't original. Regardless of who did what first – and aside from hefty legal bills and a lot of stress – you're unlikely to make any impact if you have a product that's been seen before.

Some might argue that if you compete on price, offering a cheaper alternative to what's already out there, you can still be successful. Of course, in some instances this may be the case, but this will only be sustainable in the short term. There is no loyalty, and if someone undercuts you, your business model is in tatters. And then what happens when you want to make something else? How do you differentiate if not on cost?

Once you've learnt more about yourself and what makes you really different from all the other creative makers, ask how you will stand out and grab people's attention with something new and exciting. I find looking at what's happening in the world and what's missing a huge help. Seek out the sweet spot between what's special about what you do and what customers want – which needs aren't already being met? Keeping on top of things such as trends, new technologies and what the industry is up to, while staying true to what's special about your brand, can all help focus the mind when it comes to finding your own niche.

YOUR BRAND'S PERSONALITY

Now think of your business as if it was a person for a moment. Would you want to be friends with them and why? What is it about them that you like: do they make you laugh, do you have loads in common, do they make you feel good about yourself? It helps if your customers can get to know the company beyond the work. Of course, what you make is the number one priority, and any business, no matter how good the brand, will struggle in the long term if what they do isn't well made and appealing to its audience. But think about how powerful your business could be if you got all that right, and got people following what you did and wanting to be a part of it, feeling they had to have the next piece of work you create before they've even seen it because they know it will embody the same ideas that they love about all your other designs.

WHO IS THE CUSTOMER?

Now you need a deeper understanding of your target market. Once you've pinpointed who you would like to buy your work, it's worth really getting to know them: where do they live, shop and hang out? What kind of magazines do they read, what music do they listen to and what's their personal style? Build a picture (perhaps literally – using a mood board to illustrate the answers to those questions) of this ideal customer and then seek them out. Put your work and your ideas in front of them and see if there is a fit.

BRAND AS A BLUEPRINT

Once you have figured out what makes you tick, get it all down on paper. I always find it helpful to define a business in a sentence, a paragraph and a page. This isn't something you have to share publicly or have as a tagline, it is more of a blueprint for you. I always try to keep HAM's principles rattling around in my head as a checklist for everything I do. Your brand is not just useful for figuring out how your website should look or for generating your 'about' copy, it can act as a guide when it comes to deciding a whole host of things connected to the business, such as:

The kind of places you want to sell your work: when talking to retailers and booking stands at shows and markets, ask yourself whether they sell similar brands, have the same values, reach your audience and tell their story in line with how you want to tell yours.

The type of people you employ or get to help you: this is really important because when you are not around these people are ambassadors for your brand, so make sure they fit with how you want to be perceived. Do they share your spirit and understand your story? For example, one brand may be thoughtful and understated, while another may be bubbly and outgoing and the personalities involved should reflect this. When you start getting

people to sell on your behalf, do your PR, or run workshops, it's definitely worth sitting with your brand principles when you are writing the job description or brief.

The kind of products you're going to make: it's so easy to get distracted by what other people are doing, or by new technologies, fads and trends. But if you come up with new ideas using your brand as a starting point, they will tie in with the rest of your work, be unique to you and resonate with the people you want to sell to.

The way you tell your story: many brands no longer worry about being absolutely consistent – it's really hard, and not very interesting, to make things exactly the same all the time. What's important is that people understand the personality of a business, that they can relate to it and that they want to be a part of it. It's therefore worth making it easy for people to connect with what you stand for. Talk about it on your website, show it on your packaging, weave it into all your social media channels, share behind-the-scenes videos, and blog about like-minded design.

YOUR NAME

This is a crucial element to your brand. I often get asked where the name 'HAM' comes from. It is in fact my family name and was very handy as one of my first protagonists was a pig. Coming up with a name is tough. So many have already been taken or the URL or social media handles aren't available, which is pretty important when it comes to promoting your brand. Using your own name is a straightforward route, but may cause problems later if the business grows beyond you.

Opting for a made-up word or a phrase is another popular way to get something original and good for search engines. Whatever you go for, check with the UK Intellectual Property Office to make sure there are no potential trademark conflicts with other businesses. And don't forget to test it in other languages. You don't want to have to change it when your business goes global.

TEST AND TEST AGAIN

It's easy to get lost in an idea, especially if you've spent months working on it. You know the back story, the love and the labour, but when it comes to someone else buying it, they may only have a couple of minutes to make a decision about whether or not they want what you've made in their life!

I can't stress enough how important it is to get your work in front of people throughout the creative process and absolutely before you launch it publicly. Friends and family were keen to help me, but I had to impress on them the need to be honest! They've seen you slave over your creation for months and might not want to say anything that will rock the boat, so perhaps get them to ask a friend too – someone a bit more removed who can be really objective. This can be a bit daunting, and the last thing you want to hear is 'I don't get it' or 'It's rubbish', so be prepared by giving them a list of tailored questions. Get them to rank the work in order of preference and give reasons. Let them live with the concepts for a couple of days and see if their opinion changes. Ask them to share which elements they connect with, who they would buy it for, what they think the idea behind it is and any changes they would make to improve it. Most people love to share their opinions and in return you will gain one of the most valuable business tools for free.

TRY NOT TO BE DRIVEN BY CASH

It's so hard trying to pay the rent and start a business. If someone is offering to sell your work that's great, but it's important to find out exactly how and where this will happen, and understand as much as you can about the process to ensure it fits with your brand. When you are starting out, everything you are involved in can define you, so think hard about who to partner with and whether they are going to tell your story in the right way. It's no good working with a bargain store if you want to position yourself as a premium product.

YOU ARE THE MASTER OF YOUR OWN DESTINY

I've been fortunate to meet loads of amazing designers, makers and illustrators and one thing I can confidently say is pretty universal across all those still going strong is that the team or individual behind each idea has worked really hard to make it happen. Long nights writing web copy, early mornings setting up trade stands, the regular rearrangement of living rooms to accommodate stock and the constant review of collections and product ranges all seem to be standard scenarios for the modern entrepreneur. This state of controlled flux is exciting and exhausting at the same time, but with the rapid evolution of technology, culture and creativity, brands always need to keep one eye on making sure what they stand for and how they are different is still fresh and relevant.

It is really hard to create new work and be original, especially when anyone can access artwork from anywhere in the world. But with this global marketplace come huge opportunities. Technology is an enabler for business and allows you to tell your brand's story to a worldwide audience like never before for very little money and very big returns. This is a great time to be a creative and if you can make something brilliant, original and different, and tell people about it in an authentic, meaningful and emotive way, they will soon be clamouring for a bit of what you do!

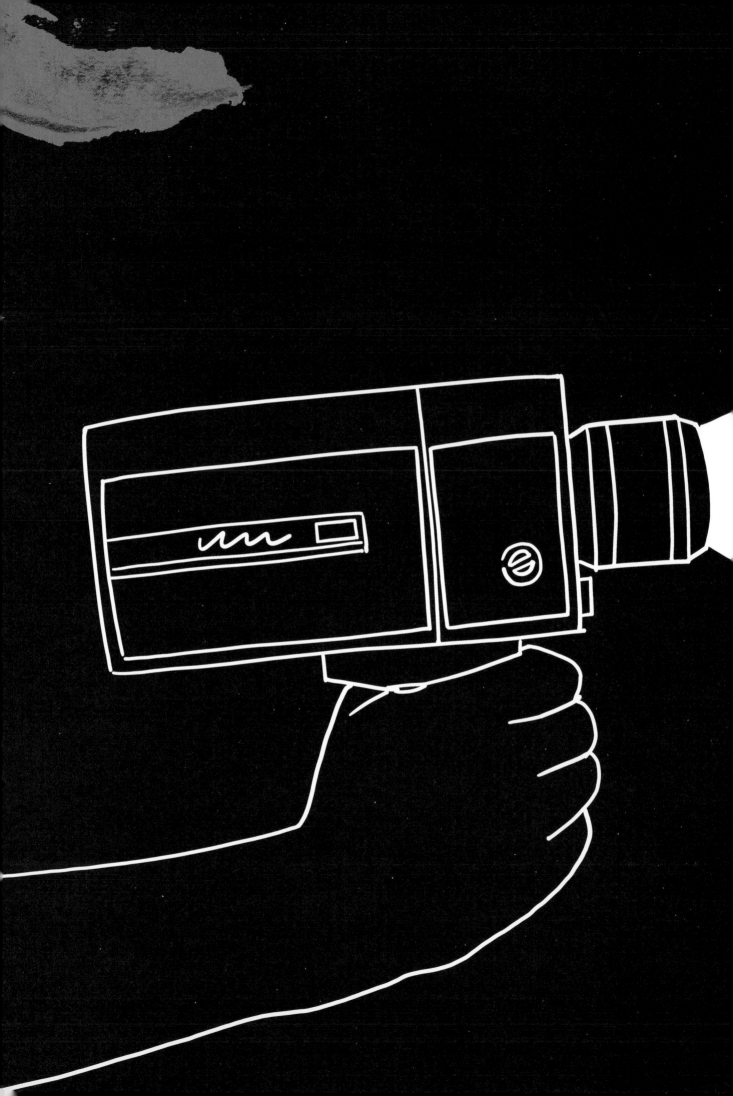

HOW TO PUT ON A SHOW

KATE HIGGINSON
HOW TO PUT ON A SHOW

After graduating with a BA in costume design from Central Saint Martins in London, Kate Higginson worked with oscar-winning costume designer Janty Yates for seven years. Higginson joined Print Club London in 2008 and oversees all aspects of new business and development of the screenprinting house. She works directly with clients such as Stella McCartney, Nike, Soho House, Twitter, the Tate Gallery and Facebook HQ. Higginson's role focuses on collaborations with brands and showcasing artists commercially. Together with Fred Higginson and Rose Stallard, she has co-curated a number of shows, including the acclaimed *Blisters* series and film poster exhibitions, which were part of the Film4 Summer Screen at Somerset House.

CURATING AN EXHIBITION OF WORKS

Now you have produced your prints, it's time to sell them. Curating exhibitions is costly, time consuming and hard work. The amount of preparation you put into any exhibition, small or large, will show. This is the opportunity for your work to meet its public and for you as an artist to get one-on-one feedback from your buyers and friends. This is your chance to talk to people about your work, so make the most of it.

THE BIG IDEA FOR AN EXHIBITION

When curating a show the first step is to come up with the big idea. You need to think about whether it's going to be a solo show or a group show. Are you going to restrict the work by size, or by format, or by the number of colours used? Sometimes if you give yourself a brief before you print the work, it helps to give it direction and the overall look you are after is easier to achieve. It can, of course, just be a collection of works, for instance, a year's worth of printing. Or it can be a collection specifically curated for this one show.

For our very first *Blisters* show we briefed each artist to produce a print at the same format, 50 x 70 cm. We chose the same size format as we wanted uniformity across all prints at this particular show. We also hoped it would become our trademark annual exhibition and therefore a key element was size of print, edition size and price.

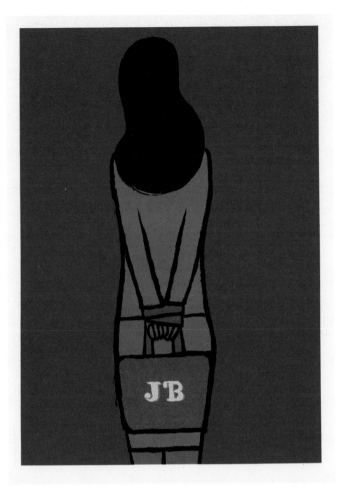

Jean Jullien, *Jackie Brown*, Summer Screen exhibition at Somerset House, London, 2016

Joe Wilson, *Princess Mononoke*, Summer Screen exhibition at Somerset House, London, 2015

All the prints were the same price, £50 each. We commissioned Eine, Pure Evil and many more established artists and designers to take part and asked that all the prints be sold at the same price. It allowed us to put everyone on a level playing field, from up-and-coming designers to the greats.

You don't have to stick to this rule, but we found that when our customers weren't driven by higher price points they were free to explore the work and be driven by creative preference. It allowed us to get an insight into our buyers and their demographic, and this very much shaped the way Print Club grew. From this first exhibition we knew quickly that our buyers liked affordable prints and as most of them were young professionals price point was fundamental. But, most importantly, they were excited by the variety of work, many of them buying more than one print.

So, where do you start?

SETTING A BRIEF

You may be working on a solo show, but to define your direction it can be helpful to write yourself a brief. This can define the size of papers, the format, the colour choices and the number of colours used. If you're working with other artists, it can be helpful to produce a brief that clearly and concisely explains what you want them to produce.

SOME KEY TERMS

A limited edition is where the number of prints is restricted to a specific quantity chosen by the artist. The prints are usually numbered. Once the edition is sold out, no additional prints will be made or be available to sell. The limited-edition aspect of a piece of art will make it more valuable and desirable.

An artist's proof is a designated set of identical prints outside of the numbered copies in the edition which are retained by the artist or publisher. They are treated separately from the numbered edition and sometimes are more valued than the actual edition because there are even fewer of them.

Printer's proofs are identical prints to those of the edition, but are the property of the printer responsible for printing. As with the artist's proofs, they are sometimes more sought-after than the actual edition.

CHOOSING WHO YOU WANT TO WORK WITH

Whether you are working alone or with a collective, it's key that everyone is on the same page and happy to have discussions. Collaboration is the key. Be open to ideas and ask for feedback and input from friends or colleagues if you are working alone. Someone else will always notice something that you might not have done and this could be an integral element to your show.

With *Blisters* we send out a submission poster and a brief, and hundreds of people send us a draft image. We then choose those that will work best as a screenprint. We receive lots of incredible designs, but some just don't work as prints, so we choose the works based on a number of factors.

We don't put too much emphasis on just selecting established designers; it's about the strength of the design and whether the work is a great example of design. Emerging illustrators can produce designs that are equally impressive.

We look at each piece and think about whether it works well with the other prints selected. Curation is important to the look of a show and we have several rounds of feedback between all of us where we lay out selections and ensure that the best set is chosen.

THE MARMITE REACTION

While it's important to curate together there's also one exception to the rule. We call it the Marmite reaction. When we review the pieces together and start looking at the show as a whole we want to ensure we love the prints. However, it's also important to remember that as a team we have very different tastes. If people feel indifferent about a print, then it's likely that our customers might too, but if one of our team is totally blown away by a print, even if the rest of the team really dislike it, then we consider this work to be a contender.

We always want the prints that get chosen to be ones we feel passionate about. It doesn't matter if we disagree, but it does matter that we feel strongly about them and that they are exciting pieces. We never want to pick middle-of-the-road prints – we don't always want to go for the safe option. Occasionally, there will be one print that provokes the Marmite reaction among our team and these prints can prove to be big sellers.

You can't learn how to have creative intuition. It's something you either have or you don't, it's an instinct. And to trust in this is the most valuable commodity any artist can have. If you love it, then there's a good chance someone else will too.

FIND LIKE-MINDED PEOPLE

One thing we have learnt over the years – and it's been the biggest learning curve of all – is that it's important to find people who are like-minded. If you have the same goal, then it's much easier to discuss a print without fear of the artist's response. We've been sent works in the past that may not have been quite as finished as possible – we felt they missed a little 'something'. If you have a good relationship with an artist, where you can openly discuss something, then it's much easier to broach subjects such as changing a design or asking for a completely new submission. We tend to work with some artists year on year as they understand the ethos of Print Club. This is key to getting the best work and putting on a successful show.

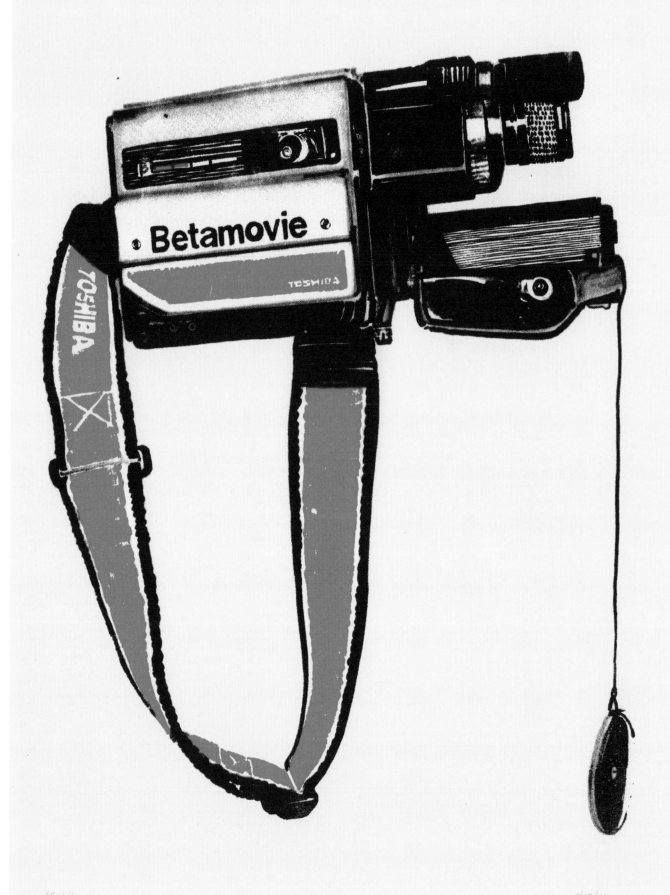

Holly Wales, *Betamovie*, Secret Blisters show, 2009

Hattie Stewart, *Surfboard*, Blisters: Sound Sessions, 2014

GETTING THE WORD OUT THERE

Telling people about your show is much easier in the modern day with social media, although we still go down the old school route and paste-up posters and flyers.

Ensure you have a show poster that tells people about the event, giving the key details. Get your friends to help you and put posters in local cafes, art shops and anywhere you think someone might see it. Blogs relating to your shows can also be really helpful. When we set up a film poster exhibition we went onto big blogs for film buffs and added our poster. This will start a buzz around your show and it also encourages online sales if you have a website to sell the work.

Make sure you know your buyers. When we were putting our film poster show together we discovered through Google Analytics that many people who liked our show images or were following our Instagram posts were in the US. It was important for sales that we made sure they knew that the prints were available online and could be shipped worldwide. Unless you tell someone then they won't know. Never think it's obvious because it may not be.

THIS IS THE ONLY PLACE

I AM HAPPY

A.B.

Anthony Burrill, *The Way Way Back*, Summer Screen exhibition at Somerset House, London, 2014

HARNESS YOUR ARTISTS

If you are doing a group show, then it's a group effort. We always ask our artists to be a big part of the promotion – many hands make light work. They should all invite guests, promote the project and get out there to put up posters.

Don't forget your show poster should include the following:

DATE, VENUE, ARTISTS and a strong visual that attracts people.

PROMOTING AND PUBLICIZING YOUR EVENT

We have worked with agencies on a couple of occasions to promote shows, but overall our experience is that nobody knows your audience better than you. And nobody is as driven to make something a success as you. Our best results have always been when we've done it as a team together. So be prepared for a lot of legwork. Promoting an event is the hardest part of all and takes time.

TIMELINE FOR PRESS

Getting your event in the press takes time and forward planning. Promoting your event is the most important part of your job once the curation is done. Ensure you make note of timelines early on because they approach quickly.

PRESS RELEASE CONTENT

Never write 'press release' as the subject line for PR.
Give key info on the project with the details at the top. The key info should only include what you are promoting:
- A short subheading
- Key dates
- Summary information
- Keep to the facts and make it modest, but positive
- Use successful superlatives (e.g., largest ever, first ever, most popular)
- Include further information on artists and the gallery
- Details of any sponsors – this is very important and often something sponsors will be grateful for or even require

KEY PRESS MATERIALS
Press images:
Select three to five images and no more than seven. Use your strongest work or the most well-known artists. There's no harm in using the big names to get people to a show and then you can showcase all the talent.

Successful press images tend to be bold and colourful.

"I'll be right here..."

Rose Blake, *E.T.*, Summer Screen exhibition at Somerset House, London, 2014

275

James Joyce, *Beauty Spot*, Secret Blisters show, 2009

MEDIA KIT

Putting together a media kit is a great way of really defining what and who you are in a few sentences. It should include information about you or your company, artist profiles, contact information and anything else that will give the reader an insight into who you are and what you do. There are no rules about how to make a media kit – each one is different. It's important to remember, though, that however familiar you are with your company, journalists may not be. Our media kit even describes the screenprinting process. We edit ours on a yearly basis and it helps to look back at what you wanted to achieve and ask yourself if you have done that.

PITCHING TIMELINES

Long-lead titles: four months in advance. This usually includes glossy magazines such as *Elle* and *Vogue*.
Mid-lead titles: two–three months in advance.
Short-lead titles: four–six weeks in advance. This usually includes weekly magazines.
Online: two weeks is usually enough.

RYCA, *Back to the Future*, Blisters: The Director's Cut, 2012

Peter Strain, *Pink Rabbits*, Blisters: Sound Sessions, 2014

Mr Bingo, *Charlie Does a Kick Flip*, Blackout Blisters, 2010

PITCHING TIPS

Get the name of the person you are pitching to right (this is obvious, but people often get it wrong).

Know the magazine: which slot are you emailing about? Why is the project suitable?

Know the target audience.

Always put a date in the email.

PROFESSIONAL FRAMING

Decent frames really help sell a piece of work. Even if it's low-cost artwork it will look better in a bespoke frame. If you can't afford a wooden frame, then go for a good aluminium one.

SELLING

People who come to shows want to buy, so make the process as easy as possible. We set up a tick list system for *Blisters* – each guest was provided with a tick list of artists' names and a pencil. As they toured the show they could mark any prints they liked and then bring the list to our shop for collection. Guests never remember names so make it simple for them. This will encourage them to buy. If you have a smaller volume of work, make sure all the works are priced. People are nervous to ask for a price in case they can't afford something. Make sure you label your work clearly and neatly.

OPENING NIGHT

Hopefully all of the above worked and you have lots of guests at
your show. We run RSVPs via apps for our events. The event is
open to all and is free but it's a good way to keep track of numbers,
especially if your space is small. Likewise, if you have a large space
and only 50 people have RSVP'd then you need to work a little
harder at your promotion. By using an app you also capture key info
such as buyers' emails. This means you can contact them after the
show – aftersales can be just as significant as those on the night.
Likewise, you can keep people in the loop about your future shows
and use this information to build your mailing list. Working as an
artist can be a solitary job and exhibitions really are the time when
you finally get to talk about what you have been doing and watch
people as they dip into and enjoy the fruits of your labour. Step back
and watch. We've learnt the most from ear wigging and chatting to
our buyers and friends. Don't be afraid to talk to people about your
work. Our shows are often the highlight of our year and enjoying it
with your team or your friends makes all the hard work worthwhile.
Remember to have a beer and celebrate!

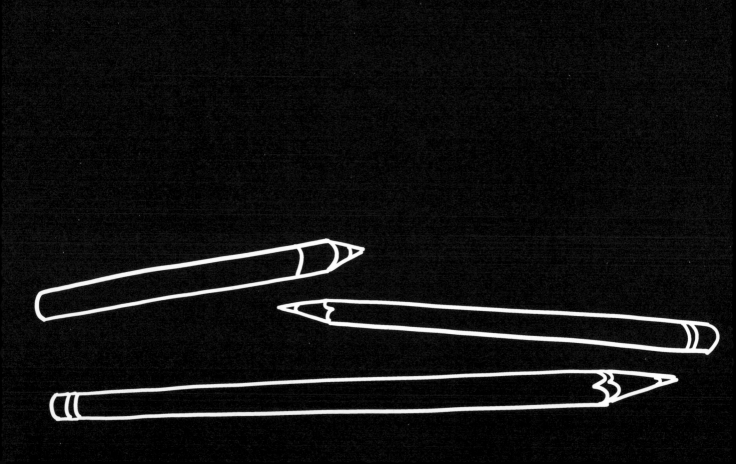

THANK YOU !

Authors

Fred Higginson
Kate Higginson
Rose Stallard

Co-authors

Amber Henry
Elliot Kruszynski

Photography

Julian Love

Photography Assistant

Katie Rollings

Illustrations

Rose Stallard

Printers for the book

Sam Baldwin
Louis Carpenter
Josh Cole
Chris Murphy
Stephanie Unger

Contributors

Danny Augustine
Sam Baldwin
Adam Bridgland
Dave Buonaguidi
Louis Carpenter
Julia Class
Lucille Clerc
Joe Cruz
Donk
Ben Eine
Guy Gatier
Kate Gibb
Bob Gill
Matthew Green
Jo Ham
Marco Lawrence
Andrew Leo
Lovenskate
Ministry of Love
Chris Murphy
Ornamental Conifer
Anthony Peters
Pure Evil
Ben Rider
Rob Ryan
The Soft City
Stephanie Unger
Thomas Whitcombe
Caspar Williamson
Steve Wilson
Susie Wright
Cassandra Yap

We would like to thank...

Screen Tec Print Essentials Ltd, for the advice on mixing inks and supporting some of our mad ideas.

G . F Smith, who have supported us on so many projects over the years with their paper. You guys are the best and our shows have only been possible with your support.

John Purcell Paper, for supplying us with paper for our workshops year on year.

Martin Field, the co-founder of Bluetack Collective with Fred Higginson. Your part in the founding of the arts charity made all of this possible.

Castle Gibson, our incredible neighbours. Your support and loan of the beautiful M C Motors has made our *Blisters* shows achievable. We are indebted to you.

Our technicians who have worked with us on the book in the studios: Claudia Borfiga, Rozalina Burkova, Louis Carpenter, Simon Fitzmaurice Oli Fowler, Indra Gersone, Rose Electra Harris, Craig Keenan, Sophie Kirk, Alice Kiteley, Barry Leonard, Aleesha Nandhra, Joe Nava, Pawel Nyszczyj, Francesca Tiley and James Willsher.

Siân Bolton and Cara Bray in the office who have kept the ship afloat and prints flying out the doors to our customers.

We hope we inspire you to go out there pick up a squeegee and get printing. Any space can be turned into a print room and any idea can become the biggest seller of your career.

This book is for all our technicians and our team at Print Club who have been loyal to us over the years. You have challenged the realms of printing, learned about new trends, created ideas and inspired an ever-evolving generation of inky printers. Your commitment to the frequent madness of our studios and your love of screenprinting never fail to amaze us. Print Club was created by us, but is run by you and your incredible passion and skill. You, the technicians and the team, have built this fantastic machine. Thank you. Thank you. Thank you.

An enormous thank you goes to Amber and Elliot, our dedicated gallery manager and studio manager, who have co-written this book. You have both worked tirelessly to produce this beauty of a bible – without you it would still be a pitch document in an ever-growing pile of ideas.

And, lastly, to our parents for supporting us through art school. We did OK, didn't we.

With love
Fred, Kate and Rose

HAVE FUN AND SPREAD THE INK!

PRINTCLUBLONDON.COM